CW00848395

Pet Rats

How to Easily Train and Care for Your Ratties... To Have a Happy Life Together

By Colin Patterson

ISBN 978-1-84728-570-6

Cover art by Landrum Creations. http://www.landrumcreations.smugmug.com/

Disclaimer
This book is for informational and entertainment purposes only and should not be considered professional veterinary advice. If you have health questions for your pet rats, consult your veterinarian.

Praise for *Pet Rats* By Colin Patterson

"Colin, I really liked your book because it taught me what I need to know to train my little babies. I've already taught them all the stand command. It was really cool when my friend came over today and saw my rats stand in unison"

- Jennifer Douglas
New York, NY USA

"Your book is well organised and easy to understand. I like that it covers all, from the right cage, to how to train, to how to feed. I learned a great amount from your book and wish you the best of luck, Colin."

- Michael Martin
London, UK

"Hi Colin,
Three months ago I purchased a pet male rat I call Freddy. At first he was very aggressive. He was nipping me and he was a little crazy. I grew to really care for him. The moment I purchased your book. Everything changed for the better. I used all your tools. All he does now is kiss me. I was thinking of getting him a mate. I am a Little afraid of getting a female in fear she will get pregnant. I am also a little scared to get a male thinking they will fight. Freddy is about five months old. Maybe it would be best to just leave well enough alone. I really appreciate your opinion. Your book was a real life saver for Freddy and I.I tell everyone who has a rat they have to buy your book.

Thank you Again"
- Shannon Brancato
Oceanside, California

Contents

INTRODUCTION: WHY RATS ARE THE NEW SENSA-TION!

I've been a keeper and breeder of pet rats for almost three decades now. From the early days of the hobby's humble beginnings, I've been overjoyed to see the explosion of popularity of ratties over the past couple of years, thanks in large part to the Internet.

What first got me so interested in rats was their amazing antics. I was amazed at how so much personality could be balled up in such a small animal. When I first went to my friend's house that fateful day in 1978, my heart melted when his rattie grabbed my pant leg with his little paws, and my friend told me that the rat wanted me to pick him up. I picked him up and the rat nuzzled his nose in to my ear...and I was hooked for life.

Rats, in my estimation, make the best pets no matter how you look at it. They've got as much personality and love for people as any dog, yet they don't need to be taken on walks. They're about the same size as hamsters, mice and gerbils and just as inexpensive to take care of, but they don't have that nasty tendency to bite. They're as cute as cats – but many cats don't like to cuddle, and cat food and kitty litter can be expensive. And unlike with dogs and cats, there's no need to take your rat for expensive regular veterinary check ups.

Rats have it all. They're fun, love people, and don't need a large living area. They love you to death, always wanting to snuggle with you or play. They're also entertaining – you can sit back and watch rattie antics all day. With one look, you know they can read your mind – and that they already love you. (Rats are highly intelligent!)

When you have a rat as a pet, all you need to do is love them. There's so little work involved, and they give you a tremendous amount of joy in return.

1. KEEPING RATS AS PETS

Despite all the bad press, rats are increasingly being chosen as pets. Never mind the popular images of domestic damsels in distress climbing on kitchen chairs while shrieking "Eek! A rat!" Forget all the rumors you heard about filthy vermin scurrying about, populating sewers and spreading diseases. If you ever experience the privilege of taming, keeping, and befriending domesticated or fancy rats, you will quickly forget all the urban rat legends you ever heard.

Interestingly enough, not all cultures fostered such distaste for these rodents of a species called *Rattus norvegicus*. Historically, rats were loved and even revered in regions throughout Asia where folklore paints a favorable picture of intelligent, playful, and mischievous creatures.

Rats are HIGHLY intelligent!

The earliest documented case of rats bred in captivity comes from 19th Century England. Over 100 years of selective breeding has resulted in today's domesticated rat, no more similar to its wild predecessor as dogs or cats would be to theirs. Today, fancy rats continue to be bred and many are even trained to compete in shows.

As tame as they are, these furry little animals have retained their natural tendencies to dig, climb, swim, and search... and of course, to chew. Therefore, the more "rat-proofed" your home is, the more play space your pet will have.

Contrary to what many may believe, rats are clean, evidenced by the fact that they will readily (and perhaps obsessively) groom themselves and each other. In fact, grooming is an integral part of their social behavior.

When kept properly, today's rats are typically docile, tame, and adaptable to new people and environments. They will not bite. However when extremely threatened, as in cases of pregnancy or abuse, they may resort to such defensive behavior. Young rats may occasionally nip on fingertips, particularly if they smell food on them.   The bottom line, however, is that compared with other small animals such as hamsters and gerbils, rats bite far less.

Owners have found rats to be highly intelligent creatures that are easily trained. Your rat will learn to approach you when its name is called, and for the right treat, it can learn basic commands such as "sit" and "stay." The patient and persistent rat owner of an agile and eager-to-please pet may be delighted to see his furry friend successfully complete an obstacle course of bridges, tunnels and hoops.

Although this may take weeks, even months, of consistent training the sense of accomplishment can be very rewarding for both owner and rat alike. They have proven themselves to be intelligent enough to learn a variety of things... right down to litter-training!

In time, rats can become quite fond of their owners and will welcome a ride inside a cozy pocket or perched on a shoulder. Some rats will even lick or "groom" their beloved human friends.

It has often been said that rats combine the good aspects of other pets. They offer the friendliness and unconditional love that a dog gives you. They share the cuteness and inexpensive cost of mice and hamsters. They're as clean as cats. And they're among the most intelligent of any animal, meaning they'll surprise you with all sorts of entertaining antics.

One of the few drawbacks is that rats have a typically short lifespan of two to three years on average, during which time they may be prone to tumors or respiratory infections. However, if the right precautions are taken, rats can live full healthy lives.

Keep in mind that a short life doesn't change the connection between you and your rat. It's still satisfying to have them as pets even if it's for a shorter period than you would hope. As Alfred Lord Tennyson put it,
'Tis better to have loved and lost
Than never to have loved at all.

By taking the time to learn all about pet rats, you can be assured of a positive rat-raising experience!

2. GETTING PREPARED: SOME THINGS TO CONSIDER BEFOREHAND

Allergic?

There have been cases in which people discovered that they were allergic to the dander (microscopic particles of dead dry skin) of their beloved pet. Be sure to find out before you bring them home! Use this 4-step process to find out for sure:

1. Visit a breeder or pet store for a good hour.

2. Time your visit so that you get there the day before or the day of cage clean-up.

3. Handle several rats. Let them crawl on your bare arms.

4. Breathe deeply.

Go home and notice any symptoms of hay fever, including sneezing or itching, red and watery eyes, any rashes on the skin, etc... Go back to the rats and repeat the process one or perhaps two more times. If you are exposed to their dander without any adverse effects, you are likely to be in the clear.

If you find that you are allergic, don't despair! The fact of the matter is that nothing can come between a true rat lover and her furry friends... did I say "furry"? I meant *hairless*.

That's right, hairless rats!

A genetic mutation has produced the hairless rat, and breeders have been selectively breeding hairless rats for those who wish to keep allergies at bay. While some rat lovers consider hairless rats to be a bit comely looking, others think they're "so ugly they're cute" and are thankful to be able to have fun-loving pet rats under the same roof!

Pet Store, or Breeder?

For the healthiest, sweetest, brightest, cutest, longest-lived rats, a breeder is the way to go. The role of a breeder is to aid in advancing the species of the domesticated rat. Responsible breeders will selectively breed strong and healthy rats with distinct and definable physical traits and that have positive and friendly dispositions.

For example, if a litter of babies includes any sickly rats or even one unfriendly personality, you can rest assured that they will not be bred. Therefore, with each generation, the rats become more refined in their appearance, health, and personality.

Careful breeding is a genetic science and being successful at it is not easy. Breeders must produce several generations of litters in order to come across a handful of "show quality" rats that can continue to be bred. The remaining rats will not be bred and will usually be sold as pets instead.

Oftentimes, breeders are so serious about what they do that they may have buyers sign an agreement stating that they will not to breed the rats they purchase from them.

A breeder will (and should) have an accurate pedigree for any given rat, giving you an accurate genetic history of your rat's direct ancestors. This is important for you to have if you purchase rats with the intent of breeding them. (See the bonus material "To Breed or Not to Breed.") However, being an animal breeder is wrought with challenges and responsibilities

A pet store, on the other hand, has no such responsibilities. Undesirable traits such as a predisposition to illnesses and "bad rattitudes" are bred back into the pet store rat population with each generation. Buying a pet store rat means taking risks that you will likely to have to pay for later, at the very least in veterinary bills.

Another advantage of breeders is that they can give you the rats that are right for you. For example, if you'd like a pair of rats that are particularly bright and would respond well to training, let the breeder know.

Finally, breeders tend to handle their rats often and from early on in their lives. For you, that means spending less time trying to socialize them and more time actually enjoying them. Once you bring your pet rats into your home, you should continue handling them on a regular basis—about one hour each day. Those little buddies will become close friends with you in no time at all.

Adopting a Rescued Rat?

Often your local animal shelter (as well as most breeders for that matter) will take in pet rats that had owners who for whatever reason weren't able to take care of them. The process is similar to what is would be for dogs: you can expect to find a great pet (and do a really good deed by saving a life), but don't expect to find show-quality animals or rare breeds. Also, do not expect to breed them; instead do the right thing and have them spayed or neutered.

Another place to consider rescuing a rat is from a pet store that sells them as "feeder" rats to snake owners to serve as live food for the snake. That way you'll save the rat from a frightening death.

On the other hand, however, there's the moral dilemma of financially support-ing a pet store that would have such a cruel practice. In any event, if you de-cide to go that route, keep in mind when getting feeder rats that they will not have been properly socialized, so you'll have to work with them to make him trust you.   Plus they may have health issues.

What to Look For When Getting a Rat

When you get a rat, you want to make sure that the pet you're getting will be long-lived, healthy, and friendly. Such an animal can usually only come from an environment where it is given loving care from birth. With that in mind, use the following checklist to ensure that your rattie is coming from a good source. Make sure that the answer to every one of these question is a resounding "YES!":

> - **Are you buying locally?** You want to always visit the breeder, shel-
> ter, or pet store you're getting your rat from. Otherwise you could
> be financially supporting a breeder mill or irresponsible pet store
> that has profit as its only motive – which means that many of the ani-
> mals are abused and neglected. If you're not buying locally, then at
> least do your homework to make sure you're getting your rat from a
> reputable source. Plus, you should at least try to travel and pick up
> the rat yourself. Shipping a rat can be risky.

- When checking out the breeder (or pet store or shelter), how do the other animals look and act? Are they clean? Are their cages clean? Are they stocked with fresh water? Does it appear that they are cared for? You want to make sure that the other animals are well taken care of – and also that they're friendly rather than shy and un-accustomed to close contact with humans.

- Is the person you're buying the rat from willing to answer questions? Even if they don't know everything about the rat's lineage and so forth, the fact that they're open with you is always a good sign. If you get the feeling that the person is hiding something then that should put up a big red flag for you.

- Are they asking *you* questions? Someone who cares about their rats will want to ensure you're going to provide the rats you adopt a good home.

One or Two? Boy or girl?

Rats are social creatures and thrive in each other's company. So to ensure happy pets, plan on getting a pair. In fact, most breeders will have a "two-rat rule," selling them only in pairs of males or females. Otherwise, a normally happy well-adjusted rat can become lonely, distressed, and can even be prone to illnesses.

As a general rule, males are larger than females of the same age. They tend to be the couch potatoes when they reach maturity (unless they want to mate). Overall, males are mellow, and altered males are super-mellow.

Females tend to be tinier and more hyper. Eager to scamper off in any direction, they are the most curious and mischievous. For purposes of training, females learn the quickest – but they are also most easily distracted.

Whether your pet rats are males or females, the key to success is to adopt them when they are as young as possible. Most breeders will allow their babies to go to new homes after five weeks or so.

Rat Personalities

Though there's lots of overlap, there tends to be differences between male and female rats, as I just mentioned. Boy ratties are often laid back and relaxed, while girls are likelier to be more energetic and playful. You also may find that girls are fluffier. Boys are bigger and often can create more odor problems because they mark their territory.

Unlike with other animals like dogs and cats, however, you can't really tell what a rat's personality is going to be based on its breed.

You'll hear lots of stereotypes of course. I've heard for example that dumbo rats are supposed to be calm all the time. Instead a lot of my most hyper rats have been dumbos!

In reality, rats are like people...each individual is unique in his or her own way. Breed is only skin deep. Or—to be precise—only fur deep and ears deep.

You'll also find a lot of variation in the same individual. Sylvester, my rascally, hairless boy, alternates between being spastic and running frantically around my living room...to being the most laid back lap rat you could ever imagine...lazily burying himself in my jacket as I watch TV.

Rattie Body Language & Communication

Rats are very emotional creatures, and you can read them like a book if you know what to look for.

Bruxing – This is when your rat grinds his teeth and sometimes blows air out of his mouth at the same time. Your little guy does this when he's happy, much like how a cat purrs. By the way, don't worry – it's normal and healthy for your rats to grind their teeth. Rats' teeth never stop growing, so they must keep grinding them down.

Ear flapping – Done by females in heat. Often accompanied by arching her back to put herself into a prone position. When your little girl flaps her ears, keep the little boys away unless you want a bunch of little rattie kittens!

Rubbing themselves on things – Often your rat will rub his body along the walls of his cage or rub his feet on the cage floor. This is your rattie's way of saying, "This area's mine!" Sure, it means your rat's being territorial. Still, when you see this, be happy. It means your rat feels at home.

Head swaying, lying down – When he's in unfamiliar surroundings (such as when you first bring him home), your rattie may lie on the ground and swirl his head around like Stevie Wonder rocking to a smooth groove...even though there's no music! Your rattie does this in order to see better, since his vision is very poor. He's nervous and a little frightened, but when he becomes familiar with the situation, he'll stop.

Head swaying, standing up – Your rat does this to get a good whiff of his surroundings.

Eye boggling - This is when your rat's eyes appear to pulsate up and down, a phenomenon caused by the movement of his jaw. Like bruxing, your rat does this when he's happy.

Licking - Often, when you're having a nice moment with your happy rat, he'll start licking you. Don't worry about this. He's not about to bite you. He's just grooming you, which is a sign of affection. When rats are happily living together, you'll see them grooming one another. It's the same thing with you!

"I love you! (And now your finger is as cute as I am!)"

Signs of aggression - When you see a rat (usually a male) displaying the following, watch out: fur standing up, making the rat appear to be bigger; teeth grinding hard (more forcefully than when they're bruxing); ears flat; making a hiss; tensed body; firm glare; and baring teeth.

Displays of dominance - Like most (perhaps all?) other social animals, ratties too have a pecking order. An alpha rat will roll the less dominant beta rat on his back. Then the alpha will sniff the beta up and down before releasing him. Sometimes this ritual is accompanied by a play fight.

Sleeping stretched out - Your rat's normal sleeping position is curled up in a ball or snuggled up with other rats. If you notice your rat sleeping on the bare floor of his cage with an out-stretched body, it means he's too hot. Lower the temperature.

Short, quick squeaks that make your rat's body shake   This confused me for the longest time. Was my rat telling me she was nervous? Was she laughing with joy? Then it hit me: these are just rattie hiccups. Usually rats get them when they've had a little excitement such as just waking up from a snooze.

Different Breeds of Rats

Rats have officially been bred in England since the turn of the 20th Century. Since then, various breeding methods have produced over 30 varieties of rats, exhibiting a wide array of colors, hair textures, features and markings. These characteristics show up in various combinations.

These domesticated rats became known as "fancy" (as in "I've taken quite a fancy to him"). It's just one of those British words that have an entirely differ-ent meaning in American English. When the US began importing and breeding "fancy" rats from England, the name just stuck and the American Fancy Rat and Mouse Association (AFRMA) was born.

To be a good and responsible breeder, it takes an in-depth understanding of both rat fancy standards and genetics. Otherwise, there is no way of under-standing how or why certain characteristics get passed down to future genera-tions and others don't.

As breeders strive to perfect the varieties of rats they are working with, they will always end up producing non show-standard quality types and coat colors. Unsuitable for mating, these rats will often be sold as pets. Sometimes, they may be sold to pet stores; however, this cannot be guaranteed, so use caution if you decide to get a rat from a pet store.

What is good about pet-quality rats from breeders is that they are often very healthy and extremely friendly due to the fact that they have been handled since birth. They are also better-defined, breed-wise.

Here is a brief introduction to the various colors and characteristics of the fancy rat (For more detailed descriptions of several varieties, go to "Breeding and Showing Your Best Rats.") Included in this section is a little bit of the rat-fancy history of each variety:

The Agouti Rat

This is the most common coloring in wild rats; however, domesticated Agoutis differ from their wild counterparts in that their coats are brighter, with more of a reddish hue. The first agouti rat first appeared in a show in England at the turn of the Twentieth Century in England. That makes this color over 100 years old among rat fanciers!

The Black Rat

This Agouti mutation is one of the most common in the wild. Certainly, the domesticated black rat was around long before the rat fancy; therefore it comes as no surprise that the Black has been in the show standard since the very beginning of the fancy and continues today.

The Blue Rat

This coat color is a fairly new mutation that appeared around the same time in pet stores all over the US and the UK. The first blue, a female discovered in Southern California, was found by a breeder by the name of Sheryl Leisure. She purchased the Blue doe and then carefully bred her to a Silver Lilac male, producing a new crop of Blues.

The Pink-eyed White Rat

This variety is also commonly known as the Albino. Albinism is a common, recessive genetic mutation that emerges in virtually every animal species, including in humans! While the Pink-eyed White (PEW) variety has thrived in the rat fancy, in the wild they would likely have a hard time surviving.

PEW's were among the first varieties to be bred and sold as pets in the 19th Century England. In fact, author Beatrix Potter had an Albino rat as a childhood pet and at the turn of the century she

"I prefer it indoors!"

wrote *"Samuel Whiskers,"* a children's book dedicated to this kind of rat.

In addition to their popularity as pets, Pink-eyed Whites were also among the first colors to be bred for showing. At the time of their foundings, both NFRS and AFRMA included descriptions of PEW standards.

The Siamese Rat

The great-grandparents of today's Siamese Rats were added to England's Fancy Rat Society in 1978. They hardly resembled today's Siamese at all.

However, with NFRS's breeding expertise, in time these animals developed into the Siamese Rats that we know and love today. In late 1983, the first Siamese documented by AFRMA were imported from England. Less than six months later, they made their debut appearance at an AFRMA show.

The color pattern of the Siamese rat is called acromelanism. This means that the Siamese rat's temperature will affect the color of the its fur: the colder the temperature, the darker the fur will be. Naturally, the rat's extremities (nose, ears, feet, and tail) will be cooler than the rest of it; hence, the color pattern of the Siamese.

It is for this same reason that the Siamese rat will be darker in the wintertime than in the summertime.

The Rex Rat

This curly-whiskered rat, together with the Hairless Rat, is a favorite among people with allergies to most other kinds of rat fur. It was first bred by Roy Robinson in 1976 and was subsequently standardized by the National Fancy Rat Society that same year.

Rexes were first imported to the US from England in 1983. For the remainder of that decade, breeders were busy producing the first official American Rex descendants.

The Sphynx or Hairless Rat

This perfect rat for anyone with allergies must be given special care. Keep these rats in a room no cooler than 70 degrees Fahrenheit. Also, due to their not having a coat, they are prone to getting scrapes and scratches.

The Dumbo Rat

A recessive gene causes the Dumbo to have very large and round ears that are on the side of the rat's head, reminiscent of the famous cartoon elephant. Many breeders say that the Dumbo variety of rat tends to be mellow with a stockier build. Because of both its sweet temperament and super-cute appearance, the Dumbo has been exploding in popularity in the past few years.

The Manx Rat

This tailless rat variety is usually smaller than the standard rat with front legs that are shorter than its hind legs. The manx is further subdivided into three categories:

1. The Riser—This subcategory has a very short furry tail.

2. The Stumpy—This Manx has a stump for a tail.

3. The Rump—This rare, illness-prone breed has no trace of a tail whatsoever. The Rump is illness prone because lack of a tail means it has no way to balance itself or cool itself down!

The Cinnamon Rat

Cinnamon is among the oldest standardized colors in the rat fancy, both in England and the US. This variety is produced when a **Mink** (or **Lilac** in AFRMA) Rat is bred with an Agouti rat. The official age of this color is uncertain because at the turn of the 20th Century, Minks were, for some reason, being recorded as "Blue." This has resulted in some confusion as to the exact time of its origin.

In the 1920's, this Cinnamon Rat was first known in the UK Fancy as "Fawn Agouti" but the name was eventually changed in the NRFS to Cinnamon in 1976. By the late 1970's, other Mink Offshoots such as **Cinnamon Pearl** and **Pearl** emerged in the standards.

The first hooded Mink was discovered in a US pet store in May of 1978. This male rat was named "Hershey" and during his lifetime he took part in producing Lilac, Cinnamon and **Silver Lilac**. Fanciers were to later discover that Lilac and Mink share an identical genetic code with only a slight difference in shading.

The Satin Rat

A rat with a coat that is thinner, silkier and shinier than other varieties. It also has distinctive whiskers. The Satin is rare because it is hard to breed.

The Dwarf Rat

This rat is usually about the size of a gerbil.

The Velvet Rat

This breed is related to the Rex, but with much shorter and crimped fur.

The Hooded Rat

A Hooded Rat can be of any color. Their history predates the Fancy all the way back to the late 1800's. Rat historians suspect that this marking was first described as "black and white even marked" at a show around the turn of the 20th Century. From there, the name changed to "Japanese," then "Japanese Hooded," then "English Hooded" and finally "Hooded," the name we use today.

The reason why this distinctive color is so rare is because of the way it develops. The formation of this pattern begins early on in the fetal development of the rat. When there is a restriction in the distribution of pigment cells from the spine to its body, the result is a pigmentation pattern that forms on the head, shoulders and spine, leaving the rest of the rat white.

3. GETTING PREPARED: A HEALTHY LIVING ENVIRONMENT

Glass aquarium or wire cage?

Apart from good genes, the most important factors in the health of your rats will be their living environment and their diet. So before you bring those ratty rascals home, be sure you set up the best possible living space.

Most respiratory illnesses in rats can best be avoided by keeping their living space clean. So if you are pondering whether to keep your rats in a metal cage or an aquarium, consider the factors of ventilation and overall cleanliness.

While the glass bottom and sides of an aquarium will keep the area outside of it cleaner, the *inside* (where your rats will be living) is more likely to collect waste and contain the ammonia fumes that develop when their urine breaks down. A wire cage, on the other hand, will allow most of the waste to fall through into a tray and will allow fresh air to circulate more freely.

Furthermore, for the sake of your rats' mental health, they will need a lot of space to play and explore. While a bare-minimum sized ten-gallon aquarium can be heavy, a wire cage of the same dimensions is less cumbersome to clean out. Because wire is lighter, you could even go bigger. This would create more space for toys and tunnels and shelves and ladders. Now wouldn't your furry friends just love that?

When shopping for a wire cage, there are a few crucial things to consider:

1. Go for the biggest one possible! (90x30x30 cm. or 3'x3'x1' *minimum* for two rats).

2. Avoid galvanized metal. Rat urine will corrode this material which emits toxic fumes harmful to your rats.

3. Also, if they nibble on the bars of a galvanized metal cage (and most likely they will), they could wind up with zinc poisoning.

4. Check the spacing of the bars to ensure that little rat heads—and subsequently, their bodies—cannot get through.

5. Avoid having your little ones walk on bare metal wire. This is the most common cause of an incurable, painful condition known as bumblefoot. Also, they run the risk of getting their little feet caught, resulting in injury. Laying down smooth plastic panels or needlepoint canvas can save them a lot of agony in the long run.

6. If the floor to the best cage you can find is metal, you can easily alter it by laying down a special plastic mat or needle point canvas. In this way, urine can drain through the holes.

7. Finally, double check the latches and any other possible escape points, particularly in bird cages where the food bins can make for an easy route to freedom.

So, where will you place your rattie's "home-sweet-home"?

> - Avoid direct sunlight, as your precious ones may get overheated and die.

> - Drafts from poorly insulated or open windows are also possible health hazards. You don't want anyone catching a cold, now do you?

> - Be aware of the presence of any harsh or poisonous chemicals and cleaning supplies nearby. Remove them from the area and store them in a hidden far-away place.

Bedding

The next important element in your rat's living environment is your choice of bedding. The materials used can make a world of difference when it comes down to your rat's comfort level and how long the air will stay fresh between weekly cleanings.

There is a health concern when it comes to the use of any evergreen shavings and chips, such as pine or cedar. If the evergreen bedding material has not been previously heat-treated, the wood will contain a phenol (consisting of toxic aromatic hydrocarbons) that is likely to cause fatal liver problems and a suppressed immune system leading to respiratory issues in small rodents.

Furthermore, the dust from the shavings can also interfere with breathing.

You can either go with heat-treated evergreen bedding; however, if notice a reddish discharge coming from their noses, that is not a good sign at all. The discharge is called porphyrin and it means that the delicate tissues in their lungs and nasal passages are becoming irritated.

To play it extra safe, maple or aspen chips are good to use as bedding. Other phenol-free choices include bedding products made from corn-cob, corn husk, grain by-products, and recycled paper or reclaimed wood pulp waste.

One concern with store-bought bedding is the possible presence of tiny bugs or mites. Bugs will irritate your pet rat's skin, making life itchy and unbearable. One good tip for avoiding this is to keep the sealed bag of bedding inside the freezer for two or three days before opening it; another is to shake some cat flea powder into the bag of bedding before freezing for good measure.

Be sure to carefully examine the bedding and consider the fact that your two little babies may be breathing those particles. Another concern with store bought bedding is how fine the particles break down. Miniscule dusty particles will irritate little nasal passages and lungs, particularly when the rats burrow beneath the bedding.

This can be avoided by shaking the bedding inside of a large strainer over a sink, bathtub or garbage can. The dusty irritants will fall right through, keeping the larger, usable pieces inside.

Avoid yarn and cotton fiber bedding, no matter how soft and cozy it may seem. Babies, in particular, have been known to get caught by microscopic fibers. The consequence has been injury, amputation, and even death.

Using your old shredded newspapers as bedding may seem like a good idea, but bear in mind that newspaper print rubs off very easily. Your rat could wind up ingesting newspaper ink chemicals. Not healthy at all. However, soy ink is reportedly okay.

Finally, if you supply potential bedding material, rest assured that your furry friends will munch away and create their own bedding, in addition to the higher quality store-bought stuff. Indeed, they are veritable paper and cardboard shredders. You may use old scrap paper, used notebook paper, and cardboard box sections.

Results with freshness, absorbency, and ease of cleaning will vary from one material to another, so it's best to try different products and see which one has the winning combination for you and your little friends.

As a general guideline, here is a chart listing several possible kinds of bedding, along with some notable characteristics of each one.

Type of Bedding	Absorbency	Odor control	Healthy?	Clean-up
Cedar (not kiln dried)	n/a	n/a	NO. Toxic Phenols	n/a
Pine (not kiln dried)	n/a	n/a	NO. Toxic Phenols	n/a
Compressed pine pellets (kiln dried)	Good	Good	ok	ok
Aspen shavings	Good	Good	Yes	ok
Aspen pellets	Excellent	Excellent	Yes	Fine pieces
Maple	Excellent	Excellent	Yes	Scatter
Corn cob	Can get moldy	good	Dries the air	Messy
Newspaper	n/a	n/a	NO. Toxic ink	n/a
Reused paper pellets	Good	Varies by brand	Yes	Yes
Reclaimed wood pulp	Good	ok	ok	Fine pieces
Grain by-products	Excellent	Excellent	Yes	Flushable

Dry grass pellets	Good	Good	Yes	Flushable
Scrap cotton fabric	Good	Good	Good nest material	Easy
Denim	n/a	n/a	NO. Hazardous threads	n/a
Cotton fiber bedding	n/a	n/a	NO. Hazardous fibers	n/a
Yarn	n/a	n/a	NO. Hazardous fibers	n/a

Food and Water

When it comes to food, the two most important things to remember are to provide a wide variety of healthy, low-fat foods and to keep the food and water fresh *at all times*. Many times rat illnesses occur needlessly as a result of moldy food or contaminated water. Don't let this happen to your little babies!

Pet stores have specially formulated lab blocks that are nutritious and economical. They keep the freshest when they are stored inside of an airtight container. Lab blocks can be a better choice than seed mixes – since the variety of grains are compressed, your little wise guy won't be able to pick out his favorite foods and leave his least favorite morsels for you at clean-up time.

Don't forget to provide plenty of raw fruits and vegetables, including sunflower seeds. The earlier you begin to expose your rat babies to a wide range of fresh fruits and veggies, the more they will look forward to munching on them when they get older and the healthier their eating habits will be. Avoid dairy, high-fat or cooked foods. At least keep these foods to a strict minimum.

As a very general rule, there is no raw fruit or veggie that your rat shouldn't eat. That means your little one can enjoy fruits like cherries, apples, grapes, blueberries, ripe bananas, peaches, melons, apricots, tomatoes, cucumbers and bell peppers. Even avocados can be an enjoyable treat!

In moderation, your rat may enjoy all leafy greens like spinach, basil, parsley and even "weeds" from your garden such as clover, dandelion and chickweed. They also love carrots, celery, corn and anything in the cancer-fighting cabbage family like steamed broccoli, cauliflower, or Brussels sprouts.

Feed your rats nourishing food so they can live as long as possible.

Cooked, plain white or brown rice is a healthy option. Small amounts of low-fat cheese or yogurt are a favorite occasional treats. Other snacks may include unsalted (and unbuttered) popcorn, crackers, and plain shredded wheat.

If you notice rapid weight-gain, curb the high-fat foods such as nuts, seeds and hard cheeses. Obesity can become a problem, especially if they don't get enough exercise.

A few other treats include salt licks, mineral blocks and dog chews made from hide.

If you want to hand feed your ratties, that's fine. Just don't feed them through the bars of the cage. It's a bad habit that confuses them and that can result somebody's hand being bitten the next time fingers are poked between cage wires. If you want to hand feed, place your entire hand into the cage.

A chart showing which foods are "best" and which are "best to avoid" altogether:

In Abundance	In Moderation	On Occasion	Avoid
Lab blocks	Cooked pasta	Orange juice (rarely)	Peanut butter
All fruits	Cooked vegetables	Semi-sweet chocolate	Caramel
Carrots	Mashed potatoes	Cookies	Carbonated beverages
Celery	No-sugar cereals	Potato chips	Sugar/candy
Corn	Plain popcorn	Cooked meat*	Milk Chocolate
Low fat cheese	Baker's chocolate	Hard cheeses	Raw yams
Yogurt	Steamed cabbage	Hard boiled egg	Green bananas
Cucumber	Cooked squash		Raw potato
Melons	Hard cheeses		Rhubarb
	Variety of mushrooms		Raw meat
	Raw nuts and seeds		Raw cabbage
	All leafy greens		Raw artichokes

*Youngsters tend to like eating meat, while older rats will eat less of it. If they crave meat, they may need it in their diet.

Over time, you will become familiar with your little one's favorites. This will be useful information later, if you decide to train your pet to learn tricks and to run obstacle courses. However, the most recommended reward, for the sake of consistency, is a liquid nutritional supplement for rodents. (See "It's Training Time!")

Getting back to cleanliness (the key to your rattie's good health)....

In order to keep large fruits and veggies off of the ground, you must place them in holders that clip onto the bars of the cage. This will ensure that the food will stay as sanitary as possible. Be sure to remove the food when it starts to go bad, or bacteria will collect.

For tiny, loose foods like berries, you can find bins that will keep those goodies far enough above ground to keep them clean. Just line the inside with some paper towel to absorb moisture and watch out that mold does not collect during the first 48 hours after they are placed inside.

As intelligent as domesticated rats may be, they haven't quite figured out how important it is to keep their water supply clean in confined quarters. The dish will wind up collecting lab blocks, bedding, urine, and whatever else is stuck to the bottom of little rat feet and rat tails. Then, it will only be a matter of time before the dish gets knocked over, getting your rats and their bedding very wet. All-in-all, it's not a pretty picture.

For the cleanest and freshest possible drinking water, therefore, it seems that the best choice is to use a sipper bottle clamped onto the cage.

On the plus side, a water bottle stays nice and elevated... and the water inside *stays clean!* However, even so, the mouthpiece must be sanitized with alcohol or very mild bleach water each day. Otherwise bacteria will collect from the rats' soiled hands and mouths touching it all the time. Replace the old water with fresh spring or filtered water after the daily cleaning. Some rat owners even boil the water to be extra sure that there are no bacteria in it.

Water bottles can be difficult to attach and rats can sometimes chew them to shreds. To securely fasten a water bottle, you may have to get creative with wire hooks and even duct tape. Wrapping thick tape around the bottle can also be an effective method of keeping your rats from chewing a hole in the bottle. Whether you use a glass or plastic bottle is up to you. The important thing is to keep them clean and free of holes.

If you opt for glass and get unfiltered hard water build-up, you can soak the bottle in vinegar for ten minutes and then scrub it with a stiff brush.

And Finally... the Furniture!

Like children of all species, baby rats need to be able to explore and investigate to grow intellectually. Furthermore, for their mental health and stability, they need to be able to play and solve problems.

If your little guys live boring and dull lives, at best they will not be very sharp come training time; at worst, they will be neglected and unhappy. Therefore, their living space needs to be fun and stimulating to their minds.

Now, be prepared to have to replace everything within a few weeks or months. They will just chew everything in sight—even that favorite rope ladder of theirs. The reason rats have the instinct to chew constantly is that it is actually *healthy* for them; otherwise, their teeth would continue to grow impractically long, possibly leading to death. So, look forward to hearing a lot of chewing and nibbling.

Before you continue tallying up additional spending dollars in your mind for toys, stop. Most toys can be simple and inexpensive. Of course, making things from scratch is always an option. The bottom line is that creating a fun living environment for your furry friends doesn't have to cost you an arm and a leg.

You can always give your little guys plenty to chew on in hopes that they will leave their toys and furniture alone, and while doing this will minimize the damage, it will not eliminate it completely.

Here are some household items and materials that will keep your chippers and chewers busy for awhile:

1. Corrugated cardboard.
2. Milk cartons.
3. Plastic jugs.
4. Cardboard egg cartons.
5. Scraps of wood (as long as they aren't made from pine or cedar).
6. Toss in an old "ratty" t-shirt or clean-but-old rag or towel.

Rats love multi-level living environments. They will use ladders, ropes and ramps to climb onto platforms, and then they feel safe when they retreat into little burrow balls, hidey holes, bins and tunnels. So, make the cage a mini rat play land!

Exercise wheels and platforms can be easily attached to the wire walls of the cage. Just protect their tender little feet by attaching a well-ventilated cross-stitch mat along all wire surfaces. Adding hammocks and wide perches will form overpasses, creating a fun and challenging living environment for your rats.

You may need to train your rats to use some of the items, such as the exercise wheel and rope. To teach them to use the wheel, place four evenly-spaced dabs of yogurt along the inside. Watch them follow the tracks as the wheel begins to turn.

To encourage them to climb a rope, tie it to a spot that is inaccessible any other way, such as the roof of the cage. Near the top, securely attach a sunflower seed. What *wouldn't* they do to get to that seed?

How to create hiding and sleeping spots for your ratties

Simple and cheap PVC piping makes excellent tunnels. You can even experiment with various household items such as plastic bottles and containers. Be safe though. When in doubt, leave it out.

Rats love plastic plumbing pipe

When you create nests and hidey holes, remember to add at least one tiny blanket for each of your little darlings. They will appreciate a soft and cozy fleece square with an area of about 6"x6". Fleece is extra warm, and it doesn't have threads that may injure them once they get to chewing it.

When your rat isn't running around on his exercise ball, you can use twist ties to attach the ball onto the top of the cage. Place a cozy blanket inside and leave the door open for easy entry.

Home-made hammocks and balconies

A super-simple balcony can be created for your pet rat by purchasing a very tiny wicker basket (like the Easter variety) and securely fastening the handle to the top of the cage.

For a simple and disposable hammock, cut off a pant leg or arm sleeve (avoid denim, as it can have harmful threads) and thread an old scarf through it. Fasten the ends of the scarf securely onto either side of the cage.

Store-bought items

If you want to spring for it, ferret hammocks, running wheels and toys work well with rats. Hamster tunnels and wheels are invariably too small. Doll furniture can add a creative and almost human touch to their cage. If doll beds and sofas are sturdy enough, they can provide some nice soft resting spots for your rats. Ultimately, of course, *they* will pick their favorites!

A few store-bought toys can be nice to have around. Some rats will snuggle with little stuffed animals. Bird perches and toys that have bells and mirrors can provide entertainment, as well.

Don't forget the bathroom!

Contrary to what people may believe, rats really are clean animals. In fact, when given the opportunity to take a bath, they will take one; hence, the problem with giving rats water to drink from a dish. A clean rat is a happy rat, but drinking water should come out of a secure glass bottle feeder.

You may place a sturdy and heavy bowl of water inside their dwelling for the two to bathe themselves in. The bowl of water should not be left inside for more than one or two hours, as it will eventually become contaminated and is not meant to be for drinking.

Finally, save some space in the corner for a ferret litter tray or pan. Usually, rats *can* be litter-trained. They tend to leave droppings in one remote spot or corner anyway. However, they will instinctively mark their territory (the *entire* cage floor) with drops of urine. Well, one out of two ain't bad!

One way to let your rats know what the litter tray is for is by filling it with a material that is different from the bedding that will be all around their home. You may experiment with litters and even other bedding materials.

There is a wide variety of substances that will effectively absorb odors. Kitty or ferret litter is one choice. Another choice is clay, one of the most absorbent of all materials; however, the dust has been known to cause respiratory problems. For an environmentally friendly idea, try using peat moss. Soiled peat moss can easily be added to the garden soil or compost.

Getting to know their new home

Once you have everything set up, your rat will enjoy the exploration. They love playing hide and seek with treats such as sunflower seeds: You hide the seeds throughout their home, and they seek them out to eat them! This game is also great preparation for learning obstacle courses and mazes. It gets them to start using their problem-solving skills.

Finally, rats really are intelligent and they do learn quickly. So, in a matter of a couple weeks, or even in a few days, they will tire of the arrangement. To counteract this, move the furniture around every now and again to give them a renewed sense of challenge and exploration.

Just be sure to watch them carefully as they explore their new environment and as they test out any new toys. There may be health hazards that you did not anticipate. Make sure that their new arrangement is a safe one, above all.

Cleaning the cage

It's a chore that no one looks forward to. The stench and dust can be over-whelming (so just imagine how it must be for your two tender critters!) The importance of keeping a clean rat living environment cannot be overly stressed; as a matter of fact, most respiratory illnesses in rats are caused by ir-ritation from the ammonia that comes from decomposing urine, rather than by irritating dust or harmful chemicals from pine.

A little-known secret is that cage cleaning must be done once per week, and if you keep it up religiously, there will be *zero* problems with odor (as long as you're giving your rat high quality bedding and litter, of course).

Waiting a day longer than a week could mean serious infections or respiratory problems for your little guys. (See "Why did my rat die so soon?") To keep your rats as comfortable as possible in the interim, you may litter train them for solid waste management and you may also scoop up wet spots of urine (usu-ally in the corners) from the bedding once or twice a day. These actions can go a long way, but they won't entirely replace a thorough cleaning.

First, there is the cleaning aspect of the job, in which grime and waste are loosened off of the cage bars or wires. Then there is the disinfecting aspect, in which all the germs and bacteria are eliminated from the surface of the cage. A thorough cleaning and disinfecting should only take from ½ hour to 1 hour, and it is well worth the time and effort to know that your little darlings are healthy and clean.

© 2006 John Alexander Enterprises, Inc. Unauthorized duplication, copying, or transmission is prohibited.

Here is a step-by-step, quick-and-easy method for cleaning and disinfecting your rats' home:

Keep your rats safe during clean-up

1. Gently place your tiny two in a small temporary cage or escape-proof box to keep them safe while the sanitizing takes place.

2. Since you will be busy with cleaning, letting them roam free and unsupervised is not a wise idea.

Actual clean-up

1. Remove any toys, mats, food trays and holders; place them in a 2'x2' plastic basin filled with a gallon of extremely hot sudsy water and a tsp. of bleach. Use antibacterial soap if you can.

2. Pick up any plastic linings or newspapers that you had placed the week before. If done correctly, the soiled bedding should get scooped up all at once.

3. In the summer, take the cage outside and hose it all down. In the winter, wet the entire cage over a large basin, or use your bathtub just before tub-cleaning time.

4. Use a stiff scrub brush dipped in water mixed with antibacterial soap to scrub any stubborn goo stuck anywhere. For extra tough jobs, car degreaser works well.

5. Once all the bars are scrubbed clean, rinse well with warm water. (You can imagine how a large glass aquarium may be a pain to clean.)

Disinfecting

1. You may use vinegar or bleach-water consisting of one-half tablespoon of bleach per gallon of water.

2. Use a spray bottle to mist the solution onto the entire inner and outer surface of the cage.

3. Air dry and do not rinse.

4. Porous surfaces, such as wood, plastic or rubber, will need twice the bleach (one full tablespoon to a gallon of water). Just be aware that the bleach will eventually destroy these materials, particularly plastic and rubber.

Back to the furniture and toys

1. Now that you've given the accessories a chance to soak, removing any solid grime will be much easier. Scrub each one with an old toothbrush. Examine each piece carefully to be sure that it is completely clean and that it is not damaged.

2. Throw away anything that is falling apart or unsafe.

3. Once they are all clean, set aside on a towel. Empty the basin and then rinse and refill with extremely hot water. Place accessories inside and rinse thoroughly. Use dish washing gloves to protect your hands.

4. Once they are all rinsed set aside on a towel. Empty the basin and then fill with a solution of one gallon of cool water with ½ tablespoon of bleach. Soak for about a minute, and then take them out.

5. Lay them out on a dry towel to drain while you return to the cage to set up the lining and bedding.

Setting it up once again

Before setting the cage up, make sure that there are no pools of water along the bottom. Wet bars will dry quickly but damp bedding will invite mold.

1. Line the bottom of the cage with sturdy plastic. Garbage bag material usually works best. Double it, if you need to.

2. Next, place a layer of unprinted newspaper (newspaper offices will sell them rather inexpensively) over the plastic lining.

3. For a more environmentally sound choice, try forgoing the plastic and use large sheets of unprinted newspaper as a liner instead. Experiment. Add a half inch layer of bedding of your choice (see "Bedding").

4. Once everything is clean and dry, place the items inside. Be sure to change the arrangement of toys and food holders. Rearrange the shelving as well.

When your rats become big litter-trained boys or girls, you may add a litter pan in the corner of their dwelling space. (See "It's Training Time!" for step-by-step instructions on litter training.) To ensure easier clean up later, line the tray with sturdy plastic before filling it with the litter.

Finally, before placing your pair of pets back into their sparkling clean home, be sure to treat them to a game of sun flower or pumpkin seed hide-and-seek by tucking some seeds away in random places throughout their dwelling. They will soon forget the whole ordeal of having been cooped up in such small quarters for what seemed like forever.

Rare instances when a rat may become aggressive and what to do about it.

As you know by now, domesticated rats are almost never aggressive animals. Whenever a rat bites or nips, it's usually caused by something – which means it's not an inherent problem with your rat, but instead a problem that's fixable. See, rats will become aggressive in certain specific instances.

Here are some cases in which rats will behave aggressively, and ways to deal with them...

Rats that feel lonely. Rats are highly social animals and like to play and wrestle with one another. Just like people, rats depend on one another's companionship to be completely happy. Deprived of that kind of company, they feel neurotic and stressed out, causing them to lash out at hands stuck into their cages!

So for the sake of your rat's mental health, always make sure to get rats in pairs. Make sure to introduce them gradually to each other, quarantining the new rat so that they could be slowly introduced rather than thrown in together. In the meantime, put a small, soft toy into the cage that your rat can snuggle with. This will at least help to ease the anxiety that your rat feels from being alone.

Rats that feel bored. Remember that rats are among the most intelligent animals in the world. Give your rattie tons of toys and things to do in her cage, so that she's able to amuse herself.

Rats that don't know who's boss. As with other social animals, rats have a hi-erarchy. Your rattie needs to know that you're the "alpha of the pack," to use dog-speak. When your rat bites you, make a squeak. Then pick him up and put him down on his back gently yet firmly. This puts him into a submissive posi-tion and indicates that you're much stronger and more dominant.

Rats (particularly babies) will sometimes bite fingers if they smell new and un-familiar food on them. Let out a high-pitched screech to let them know that it hurts! They will learn.

In the case of abuse or neglect, rats will not trust anyone and will respond very defensively. Have a lot of patience and build trust a little at a time. Wear heavy gloves when putting your hands in the cage, so that way it won't hurt when you get bitten. For three or four weeks, offer your rat treats on the palm of your flattened hand. Eventually he'll learn to link you with good feel-ings, not something threatening that he should defend himself against.

Make sure you haven't unintentionally been too rough with your rat. I've seen too many people who pick up their rats by their tails. Never do this, be-cause it hurts them.

Your rat will typically fight with a newcomer-rat to establish dominance. While this is perfectly normal behavior, do not let the scuffle go on for too long. Break them apart with a good strong squirt from a water gun.

Pregnant does, or new mothers, will normally become aggressive in order to protect their kittens. At first, allow only one trusted human to approach the babies cautiously and keep the touching and holding to a strict minimum. Be soft and gentle.

Bucks may behave aggressively when mating time comes around. Once they reach that age, there is little that can be done to calm them down. They will settle down with age; though in extreme cases, having them "altered" or "fixed" is one effective solution. Females in heat can also become aggressive. Blame it on the hormones! Again, the solution comes from spaying.

Heed this warning: rats that have been bred by a pet store can often be overly-aggressive or sickly. It is worth springing the extra 10 dollars, on average, to buy from a breeder. If it's too late, all you can do now is to NOT breed these animals.

Your rat might be sick. Even if a rat has been very loving to you, if they're all of a sudden in pain, and the pain won't go away, it can cause them to become nasty and lash out.

Your rat's cage might be too small. At an absolute bare minimum, each rat needs 1.5 cubic feet of space, with headroom of 12 inches. An easy way to expand your rat's living area is to modify the cage by adding an extra floor. You can also add an addition to the cage. Make sure of course to let your rat out to exercise. If you were cooped up in your house with nothing to do all day, you'd be stressed out too. And if some massive hand that was bigger than your entire body reached in to grab you – well, you might just feel like biting it! So don't blame your rat if he's living in stressful conditions.

Introducing rats to each other or to other animals

Rats normally get along with one another eventually, though in the beginning it's normal for them to fight and establish dominance. By the way, unlike a lot of other small rodents, rats rarely fight to the death, though they can inflict some scary looking wounds.

Introducing rats to other animals can be a risky thing to try. Rats are predatory, so if they're put in the same cage with smaller animals like mice, it's likely the rats would kill and eat the mice. (Look at it this way: you wouldn't put your cat, no matter how sweet she is, in with your pet bird, would you?) With that said, if your animals are tame and you feel pretty confident about it, go for it -- but keep a close watch at all times.

When it comes to introducing your rats to larger animals like a dog, it all depends on the personality of the dog and your rats. Some rats will play with the dog, others will be frightened and bite him, and others will go about their business as if the dog weren't even there.

You can try masking the scent of your rats or animals by placing a strong-smelling substance on them before putting them together. Experts suggest vanilla extract and a menthol ointment. Just be very careful to avoid your animals' faces, particularly their eyes.

In general, it's best if you always are in the room at the same time as your dog and rats are together, and keep them separated otherwise.

Under no circumstances should you try to introduce rats to a cat or ever have your cat in the same room with them. Cats are natural predators, and the risk of a horrible tragedy taking place far outweighs any possible benefit from having cat and rat meet.

Introducing skittish rats to humans

Occasionally, it just takes some time for rats to get used to the idea of becoming friends with a human, especially if they were not handled enough as newborns. You see, the #1 reason pet rats are shy around people is a lack of enough socialization. But the good news is that this problem is solvable. All they need is some socialization, love, and a lot of patience. Some socializing tips, tricks and techniques to make your pet rat trust you as his best friend in the whole world:

- Find an old "ratty" t-shirt and wear it all day. Place it inside the cage to give your new roomies the chance to get acquainted with your scent. Do this with another one the next day while you wash the first. Wear-and-share your shirts for a few days until your rats know who you are.

- Feed your rat by placing a treat on the end of a plastic spoon and holding it inside the cage for five minutes.

- Do this each day until your two pets begin to get over their fear of you (it may take weeks).

- When you feel that they are ready, take one rat out and hold him for about a minute. (*Never* pick up a rat by the tail. Instead, scoop up with both hands. Repeat with your other rat.

- Don't be surprised if your rats pee or poop (they do that when they're nervous).

- Wear gloves, if necessary. Gloves help because when you take your hand out of the cage in response to the rat nipping at you, you end up reinforcing unwanted behavior. But with gloves on, you can keep your hand in the cage despite being bitten.

- Talk to your rat softly and move slowly. Let no shrill sounds come out of your mouth, and don't make sudden movements.

- Once your rat trusts you to take him out of his cage, put him into a large bathrobe pocket or inside a large shirt and sit down on a couch with him snuggled next to you so that he's constantly touching you. Do this for about a half hour, twice a day. This socialization exercise makes your rat feel comfortable cuddling with you if you can do this consistently, twice a day, everyday for at least a week.

To sum up, basically you need to end up proving to your rattie that you're the loving supplier of food and affection... and that you're the boss.

Once trust is established, your rats will begin to look forward to your time together. Then, they will be ready for... *playtime*!

Introducing skittish humans to rats

Once you get to know your new furry friends, you won't understand how anyone could be afraid of your precious ones. However, the fact remains that there are people who go into a terror just thinking about rats. In some cases, it's an incurable phobia.

If you really want to share your joy, you will have to begin introducing them very slowly and cautiously to the person. Start off by just mentioning your playful pets. The more you spend time with them, the more there will be for you to gush about.

You may want to also take pictures. Be sure to show the cutest ones first. When talking about your little ratties, focus on all their positive qualities: the playfulness of their personalities, the innocence of their eyes or the softness of their fur.

It's easy to overcome people's initial questions. No, you didn't get your rattie from a sewer. No, your rattie won't infect them with black plague. No, the tails aren't gross at all — they're portable air conditioners for your pet rat that also help with balance.

If the people you want to introduce your rats to are extremely rat-phobic, then don't push the issue. Let them bring it up first. If they ask to see your pretty pair, resist the idea at first. Pique their curiosity more until they cannot stand to wait any longer.

When the moment of meeting arrives, agree just to let them see your rats. You hold them while they just watch. Make it one minute or so. If you notice they are uncomfortable, stop and put your pet rats away. Your hesitant friends or family members may need time to get used to the idea.

Each successive time, stretch the time out by a minute or so. Eventually, if they are open to it, you can invite your phobic friends to a play time session... but only if they stay calm! Truly phobic people may never get to the point where they are completely at ease around rats. At the very least, they may come to realize that rats are not as frightening as they once thought... in theory, anyway.

Rats and children

Rats are very delicate creatures, so you need to be careful when leaving a small child alone with a rattie. I had a friend whose 4 year-old daughter accidentally killed his rattie by playing too rough. It was a horrible tragedy and deeply affected both him and his little girl.

The problem is that small children want to play with rats as if they were like miniature dogs or cats and built just as tough. They'll lift the rat up and drop them. They'll yank on the rat's tail and feet. They'll squeeze the rat's body too hard. They'll wrestle with him. Kids don't do these things maliciously; they simply don't realize that they're hurting the rats.

How to protect your ratties:

1. As a general rule, kids should only play with a rat that's on the floor. Make sure your child knows not to put your rats on tables or any other high places that your ratties can fall off of.

2. Make sure your child knows not to put your ratties into shoe boxes or other enclosed containers.

3. What I'm getting at is this: The number one most crucial thing you need to do is to make your child understand that your rats are not toys! Always supervise your child when your pet rats are out of their cage. When your pet rats are in their cage, make sure your child understands that he or she is not allowed to play with them without you being there too.

4. Take small steps to make your child become familiar with your rats. At first, just sit on the floor with your child and place the rat onto your child's outstretched hand. Once he gets comfortable with that, move onto things like how to hold a rat, how to pick up a rat, how to pet a rat, and so on.

Kids also need to be taught to be careful so that they can avoid getting bitten. Make sure your children know that they shouldn't stick their fingers into the cage if their fingers have the smell of food on them. They also shouldn't stick their hands into the cage to suddenly wake up a rat. (A startled rat will instinctively defend itself—just like many people do!)

As a matter of fact, a good rule for your children to follow is to not make any sudden movements around a rat. (By the way, that's a good rule for us adults too.)

Another great activity to do early on is to have your child help you feed your rats. This helps to instill in your child's mind that rats are living creatures that need to be taken care of, not playthings to be handled roughly.

With time and proper introduction, children can become great with rats. You'll find that the bond between child and rat will become deep.

4. SUPERVISED PLAYTIME AND TIPS FOR SUCCESS-FUL RAT-PROOFING

As mentioned previously, exploring and investigating are integral to learning. This is why part of a healthy rat-life includes play time. In the beginning, however, you will only introduce them to the idea for about ten to fifteen minutes each day, because they're not yet comfortable even in their own cage yet.

Eventually (after about a few weeks), your rats should spend quality, supervised play-time outside of their home for about one hour daily.

I've found from sad experience (and from comparing notes with friends) that it's extremely important to give every rattie an hour of time outside the cage every day. It's an easy step you can take that prevents problems down the road. A rat deprived of exercise will become obese and develop a nasty temperament. (Wouldn't you if you stayed home 24-7?)

And in the long term, a lack of exercise can lead to multiple severe health problems and eventually death. Compared with that, taking a mere hour a day is nothing.

If you ever have a pair of males and a pair of females, never have them play together. After they are five weeks old they can start having babies of their own. Rats have the uncanny ability to mate with one another in the blink of an eye.

Before taking them out for play, decide on a safe and confined space in which to let them roam. The best place may be a laundry room, a mud room or a bathroom. The space should be fairly small, with little or no small spaces in the walls or floors. You might want to favor sparse flooring over furnished carpeting, as your little guys will leave urine around and may get lost behind furniture.

Keeping your rats in a small confined space will keep them safe and visible. There are those who actually allow their pet rats to roam around the house. This is usually not advisable at all, particularly during the first year of their lives when they are most curious, mischievous, and apt to get themselves into trouble. Besides, rats will deposit urine all over the place, and the areas where they typically like to do this are not the easiest to get to and clean. Get the picture?

If you want to avoid rat-proofing, you can turn any room into a rat-safe place by using a children's wading pool to create a playpen. Always stay inside with them and watch carefully to make sure they do not start chewing holes in the plastic.

If you choose not to create a playpen, then rat-proofing is essential. Much like the concept of childproofing a living space, you will be keeping your possessions safe from harm; and most importantly of all, you will be protecting your innocent little friends from hurting themselves.

Here are some tips for rat-proofing your play space:

1. Check for mousetraps and poison! Of course, *you* wouldn't. But, who is to say that the previous owner or tenant didn't? Don't find out tragically.

2. Hide all visible wires or at least wrap them with duct tape. Not only can bare electrical wires be chewed on and destroyed, but a heavy appliance on the other end of a plug dangling so much as two feet above the ground could wind up toppling down and bonking a tiny rat in the head.

3. Check doors and windows to make sure that they are closed and fully escape-proof (no gaps).

4. Remove all clothes that may be lying around, unless you don't mind seeing them with a few new holes in them!

5. Remove small objects. Remember that anything you leave out will run the risk of being chewed or urinated-on.

6. All small-to-medium-sized ingestible items need to stay out of reach. Basically, anything that would be hazardous to a 2 year-old is dangerous for little ratties too.

7. Carefully inspect air vents, corners and baseboards along the floor. Are there any gaps, crevices, open pipes, missing baseboards or molding?

8. Securely cover, duct tape, or stop up any escape routes that you may find.

9. Block off the space beneath furniture. Removing legs will work. Cardboard blocks can also work. Your rats may chew into the stuffing and get lost in there.

10. Raise or remove plants and garbage cans (or they *will* get in!).

11. Keep larger animals, like dogs or cats, out of the space!

12. Stuff an old towel or rag under the door as a temporary measure.

13. Spraying a light solution of water and cayenne pepper onto the bottom of furniture and around wires will discourage your mischievous friends from chewing.

14. If you decide on the bathroom, close the toiled seat lid and hide the toilet paper and towels.

15. If you have carpeting that you want to protect, lay down old blankets, towels or rugs that you don't mind seeing chewed up.

Setting up the play space

1. Place their litter tray in a corner just in case your little guys've gotta go...

2. Designate acceptable play space with a blanket or area rug.

3. Make a swimming pool out of a small basin by filling it with cold water up to 2 inches for larger rats. Add some blueberries to make it challenging.

4. Create a dirt box for them to dig in. Fill a 2'x2' cardboard box with soil and bury a few colorful toys to make it even more interesting for them.

5. Decorate with chewables such as scrap wire, old ratty clothes, boxing materials and threadbare towels or sheets. Your little munchkins would just *love* to nibble away at those.

6. Break out the toys!

The greatly unexplored realm of the non-caged world will surely tempt your rats' curiosities, providing you with plenty of opportunities to lay down some boundaries and train your new students to behave.

Using a spray bottle or water gun is a good way to discipline your rats, especially at the beginning. If they do something that is not okay, you can squirt them, and at the same time give a high pitched screech ending with a sharp "no!" They will quickly learn what that means and eventually all you will need to say is "no."

Once clear boundaries are established and enforced, and with frequent rewards doled out for good behavior, you can focus on playing and building trust with your gentle furry friends. This is the very first and perhaps the most crucial step in any pet-training program.

Play time!

Announce "play time!" to teach them to understand that they will get to come out and explore. Apart from the many amusements that you can prepare for your rats to enjoy, you can play with feathers, food-on-a-string, and you can even pretend your hand is a little animal and do play wrestling.

When you play different games, say a specific word that will help your rat learn what it's called. When playing feather, say "feather... feather... feather!" While wresting, say "wrestle... wrestle... wrestle!" If you do this often enough, your rat may learn to recognize specific words.

Younger rats can really enjoy playing; but as rats get older, they mellow out considerably. If your rats are more than 18 months old, they may be more apt to snuggle on your lap or in the crook of your arm and keep you company while you watch a movie. Rats are enjoyable friends in any case.

Ways to get exercise safely

Even if their home is a veritable rat amusement park, your little guys will begin to have cabin fever after being cooped up in a cage all day long. Playtime gives the little guys a chance to exercise.

How can you be sure that your terrible twosome won't be getting themselves into any trouble? There is really no way to be sure of that. Therefore, they need to be supervised in some way.

One great toy is an exercise ball. They are often made of easy-to-clean plastic and are very well ventilated. Some tips and helpful hints:

1. Only put your rats in one at a time. Never more than one.

2. Never force the ball along or roll it yourself. Let your pet rat be in control at all times.

3. If the ball has been used as a hidey hole, your rats may already be used to the idea of going inside; however, they may not yet understand that it can *move*.

4. Introduce them to the idea of running inside the ball by placing a little drop of vitamin-enhanced yogurt along the inside top of the ball. To get to it, your rat will need to shift his weight.

Another good idea is to use a harness and a leash. The advantage is that a leash increases the possibilities of where your pet rats can move around, since they will be most closely supervised. For a wonderful walk:

- Let your rat be in control and decide where to roam, as long as it is safe.

- Gently tug when she tries to go someplace that is out of bounds.

- DO NOT walk your rat in the outdoors. There is too great a risk of escaping or being frightened, if not attacked, by a bigger animal.

5. IT'S TRAINING TIME! BEHAVIOR AND AGILITY TRAINING

Since rats are such naturally intelligent creatures, they can learn many things: from basic litter training to running tricky obstacle courses. The key to success is giving them the right signals, being patient as they learn, and rewarding them profusely when they do "get it right."

Make sure that your timing is right. One of the most common mistakes people make is to begin training far too soon. In the beginning, you and your ratties will just be starting to get to know one another; there still may be some fear, anticipation or uncertainty.

The first rule of thumb is that your rat should feel comfortable with you. The friendlier he feels, the more intelligent he'll behave. It's very similar to humans, actually. Have you ever noticed how your mind seems to shut off when you're nervous (like in school when you had to struggle through a big test)? The same goes for rats.

The rat's comfort is also important so that they'll be able to take food treats from you outside their cage. Some rats will be afraid of eating from your hand when outside playing, feeling safe only when in their home, so you'll need to work with them on that first. You can do this by offering them food at their cage door, and then just outside their cage door the next time, and then a little farther out, and so on.

Get to the point where you no longer give your rats special treats when they're in the cage, but instead when they come out to play.

As mentioned before set aside time to play for up to one hour each day. Let one week go by, then another. Your little friends should know that you're one of them. No threat at all whatsoever. When your two buddies trust you and feel completely safe in your presence, then and only then is it time to start training.

For treats and rewards, try using very small amounts of their favorite food. Unsweetened baker's chocolate is a good choice. Because there is little if any milk, fat or sugar, it is actually a healthy form of chocolate for your rats.

You may want to opt for a healthier, more consistent reward for good behavior and quick learning, like a liquid vitamin and nutritional supplement. The maximum daily dose allowed for your rat (calculated by weight) can be mixed into yogurt. If they could, rats would do cartwheels for just a little drop of it. However, it is possible for your pet rat to overdose on vitamins, so be extra careful never to exceed the daily recommended dosage.

Stimulus and reward

The number one thing you need to know to understand how training works is by becoming familiar with a psychological term called "conditioned response" or "operant conditioning." What that basically means is that, with the help of a stimulus, an animal will learn to repeat the behavior that brings him a reward and avoid repeating behavior that does not.

Conditioned response is the key to everything with your pet rats. It can make them as cuddly as the snuggliest dog. It can make them obedient to your every command... and absolutely devoted to you for life.

Surely you have been doing that all along, since taking your rats out has given you plenty of opportunities to set boundaries and give them treats for good behavior. By now, you've had plenty of play time together and your rats trust you. They should be literally eating from your hand and looking forward to spending time with you each day.

Keep the training sessions brief and teach them one at a time for best results. First, let them play as usual for the first 45 minutes or so. (This is key). On the first day, designate the last five minutes of play time to rat training and work up to ten to fifteen minutes a day. This will ensure that they first get to run around, explore and enjoy unstructured play.

Another tip is to avoid giving them any food or treats during play until training begins. If they normally associate play with treats, your pair of pets will begin to wonder what happened. Furthermore, working up a little appetite will give them an incentive to learn faster.

For the first week or so, get your little guys to begin associating a reward with a specific stimulus.

First, decide on one sound (stimulus) that they will respond to while they are training. They normally respond to high pitched sounds like whistles, bells, clickers or even squeaky-toys. Whatever you decide, stick with it.

Next, decide on the ultimate favorite treat that they would do anything for. Try to give this to your rats only during training time. Just keep it healthy, okay?

You can opt to use a liquid vitamin supplement diluted with yogurt, but be careful not to overdo it. Carefully administer no more than the daily amount.

Hold the treat in one hand. As soon as your pet rat goes for it, sound the stimulus (whistle, bell, squeaky-toy, or whatever you decide). Repeat this over and over again. You may also give your pet rats kisses and cuddles... as long as it's preceded by a stimulus and is a reward that your rat will look forward to.

Remember to make training a part of regular play time. This way, your pet rat will see the sessions as fun, interesting and something to look forward to each day.

In one week, your twosome should be associating the stimulus with their reward and running to you when called (a helpful thing when they get "lost"). That's when you'll be ready to train them to do a few tricks.

Basic litter training: Step-by-step

Potty training for rats means litter training, and the sooner you begin, the better your rats will be at it, although older rats have been known to catch on quickly as well.

By the way, baby rats will usually learn litter training from a doe that already is trained, so once you get into breeding you never really need to worry about potty training again.

The key is going to come down to sounding a stimulus and giving a reward to reinforce good behavior. More on that in a minute, but first it's important to understand a rat's instincts.

A rat will instinctively leave solid waste in a corner of their enclosed dwelling, making it easy to transition them to using a litter tray.

Urine, however, is an entirely different story. Many rats, especially males, will pee all over the place in little droplets. It's a way of marking their territory and even a sign of affection. They pee on the things they like – their food, each other, and you! You can always keep an old towel or rag around to wipe up any "token of love" they leave around.

The idea of litter training is, at the very least, to get your ratties to leave all their solid waste in one spot that is set apart from the rest of their dwelling. Not only does keeping everything cleaner mean much less work for you, but it also makes the place less germy, keeping your precious pet pair as healthy as possible.

1. On cage clean-up day, notice where most of your rats' solid waste was deposited. With gloves on, pick up their solid droppings and put them aside.

2. Prepare a corner ferret litter tray with a plastic lining and then fill to about an inch to two inches from the bottom with some ferret or kitty litter. Add the droppings.

3. After cleaning the cage completely, place the prepared litter tray inside the same corner of the cage where your rats tend to leave droppings.

4. When your rat gets the idea and begins to use the litter tray, sound the stimulus and reward them profusely. Be sure to praise them with hugs and kisses, too.

5. If you see your pet rat "missing the target" you can try to move him, or at the very least, move the dropping into the tray immediately.

6. Take the time, at least once each day, to move fresh droppings into the litter tray. Eventually your quick-witted friends will notice how much cleaner and fresher the air stays when they poop in the right place.

It is also a very good idea to allow your pet rats access to a litter tray during their playtime. This would mean either keeping the entire cage accessible to them with the door open, or placing the tray in one corner of their play space.

With encouragement and rewards for good behavior, your pair of pals will be potty-trained in no time at all.

Cool rat tricks

Once your rat trusts you completely and begins to associate stimulus with reward, you can begin teaching them to do tricks.

The idea is to use a treat to coax your pet rat into doing a particular action. Then say the name of the action (which will eventually be the command that triggers the response). At the same time, sound the stimulus and deliver the reward. If you repeat the action enough times, your rat will eventually learn to associate the command with the reward, and coaxing will no longer be necessary.

Start off with simple things.

Responding to his name

Giving your rattie a treat whenever you say her name will cause her to have a good association with her name. This will also teach her to come to you when you say her name. Rats love treats, so if they know there's a good chance of getting some goodies when you say their name, they'll catch on!

Also, just as you'd do with dogs or cats, use your rat's name whenever you're talking to them, petting them, or playing with them. Never use their name when saying "no!" or in any other negative context. Remember: you want your rat to have positive associations with his name.

Coming when called

This is easy and usually is something your rats will do naturally once they've learned their names. But you can also teach your rat to respond to the command "Come here!". Start off with your rat on the opposite end of a bed, table, or some other small surface that's outside of the cage. Say "come here" and – this is key, I've discovered – pat the table top or bed at the same time. When your rat eventually comes to you, give him a treat. Repeat the process daily until your rat comes instantly.

Once your rat has learned to come to you on a bed or table, put him on to the floor and teach the "come" command there, making sure to pat the floor when you say the command. Reward him with a treat when he comes to you. Eventually you can stop patting the floor and your rat will respond simply to the phrase "come here."

Kiss

Some rats learn to love this one.

1. Put some peanut butter or yogurt (or something creamy and yummy) on your cheek or arm.
2. As your rat licks the reward, say "Kiss" over and over again.

3. Sound the stimulus.

4. Repeat until your rat understands the command "kiss."

Standing

This one's really easy.

1. Hold the reward above his head with a plastic spoon.
2. To reach the treat, he will naturally stand up on his hind legs.
3. When he does, clearly say "stand."
4. Sound the stimulus and deliver his treat.
5. Repeat over and over until he recognizes the command "Stand."

Sitting on his haunches

Once your rat learns the meaning of "stand" he will do it to get a treat.

1. Hold the spoon above him, but this time wait until he sits and say "Sit."
2. Sound the stimulus and deliver the reward.
3. Repeat over and over until he recognizes the command, "sit."

Walking on his hind legs

Follow the same steps for "sit" or "stand"... except this time, lead him away with the treat and say "walk."

Perching on your shoulder and staying in your pocket

It's fun to have your rat ride on you. For this trick, success depends a lot on your pet's age, gender, and how familiar he or she is with you. If, for instance, you just got a young female rat, you can forget about having her stay put, especially on your shoulder or pocket. In that case, you're much better off waiting at least another year until she mellows out a little. Older, socialized, male rats are best for ridin' along.

Start off with really short trips. You can encourage pocket hitch hiking if you include a soft piece of scrap cloth and bury a treat somewhere in there. If he tries to come out, gently put him back inside. After he has remained inside for a minute or two, bury another treat inside. For shoulder perching, only reward him when he stays put for an extended period of time. He'll get the idea and want to stay there longer.

By the way, you may find that when it comes to learning new tricks, your rat is ready to learn and eager to please. On the other hand, your rat may just have such an independent personality that he will just do whatever he pleases. Some rats just feel they're "above" performing for people. All you can do is try your best to teach and reward them.

Teaching your rats to play football

This is an ultra-advanced tip I learned from a British friend of mine. It may not work on every rat. (Some may be too lazy.) But if you've got the patience to work with your ratties for a long time on this, it will absolutely floor your friends who see your little ones go!

Put each rat through the following training steps:

1. Set up a little "football field" on a table, complete with a little ball. You can even make little goal at either end.

2. Place your rat on the table. Sound the stimulus. But this time, don't give him the treat until he nudges the ball. Keep working with him until he runs right for the ball, knowing he'll get a treat.

3. Now wait until your rat *pushes* the ball before you give him the treat.

4. Keep working with your rat until he pushes the ball to the goal you've set up. Eventually, your rat will know to push the ball into the goal.

5. Now place both of your trained rats on the table at the same time.

6. Make your clicking sound, and they will both try to push the ball toward the goal. Give a treat to the winner!

Fetch

This one's a simple matter of stimulus and reward, although just as with dogs, it may be easy to get them to fetch... but getting them to bring it back is the real challenge! I find the most success using things like a little wadded-up ball of paper or a small feather-covered toy. Toss it a few feet away, and your rattie will run for it. Offer him a treat to come back to you. He might or might not drop the ball on the way back, of course.

Learning a maze

Teaching your rats to learn mazes and run obstacle courses is known in the pet rat world as "agility training" and it's never too early to begin. Once their eyes are open and they want to explore, they should be given plenty of opportunities to do so.

To make a rat maze, you may use clear ferret piping. Any pipes with corners, T's, u-turns and end caps will work, but clear piping is best since you can see where your rat is at all times. Gerbil or hamster tunnel pipes are *not* appropriate, since your rat will eventually outgrow them and may get stuck.

Build the maze by fastening the pipes onto one another. Occasionally, slip a treat into the maze so that the scent will waft throughout the correct track. That will encourage your rat to follow it through to the end. After that, put one treat near the end and see what happens.

Obstacle Courses, step-by-step

If your rats' cage is a very large multi-level environment with a lot of tunnels, ladders, ropes and bridges, they will probably be agile already. On the other hand, if they were raised in a boring space, they may never get used to the idea of running the course.

Nevertheless, every rat is different with varying levels of intelligences, abilities and interests. Just keep in mind that if you want to focus on training, every bit of exposure helps. Don't keep your little guys in a medium-sized cube for a month and then wonder why they don't have the slightest interest in learning how to handle walking across a seesaw.

The key to teaching them to run an obstacle course effectively—besides using a good stimulus and reward—is to have them master the skills one at a time, beginning with the easy ones. As one skill is mastered, just add a new one to the previously learned obstacle and don't reward him until he finishes all of them. Otherwise, if your rat learns the tricks in isolation he'll be expecting a reward right after each obstacle instead of continuing to the end of the course.

One good way of building obstacles is to attach children's wood building blocks to sections of plywood with some carpenter's glue. As with *any* training, make the sessions short (no more than 20 minutes). Another tip is to switch back and forth between your two pets. The one who catches on faster can later help you teach the other one what's the trick to get that treat!

Obstacle 1: A bridge (Difficulty rating: 1)

How to build it: Using your wood blocks, build a sturdy bridge about 3" high and 12" across. For training purposes, you may want to attach some ramps to both ends.

Goal: The idea will be for your rat to climb up (perhaps attach a ramp at first), go across it, and climb down at the other end. *stimulus/treat!*

 1. Try leaving a track of blueberries or yogurt drops across the bridge.
 2. Once he gets down at the other end, sound the stimulus and reward him with his absolute favorite treat. (Be sure they get down, first.)
 3. Alternately, you can wave the reward in front of them in a spoon.
 4. Repeat it a few times, reducing the amount of coaxing each time.

Obstacle 2: A hoop (Difficulty rating: 1)

How to build it: This one may be tricky to build. Use a jigsaw to cut a circle 4" in diameter into a piece of plywood and find a way to stand it up, securely. You may also try using a small embroidery hoop or a masking tape ring.

Goal: Get him to climb up and crawl through the hoop to the other side. *stimulus/treat!*

1. Wave the reward in front of him and lead him through the hoop.

2. When all four of his feet are on the other side, sound the stimulus and reward.

3. Repeat until he goes through the hoop by himself.

Obstacle 3: A tunnel (Difficulty rating: 3)

How to build it: Glue onto a wooden board a piece of plastic or cardboard tubing.

Goal: This one may look simple—and your rat may just catch on quickly—but it has a higher rating because of most rats' tendencies to want to stay inside.

1. For this one, you may coax your rat through the tunnel by either trying the treat-on-a-string trick or the yogurt-track tactic.

2. Make sure your rat has exited the tunnel completely before sounding the stimulus and handing out the reward.

3. Repeat until he appears at the other end, asking "Hey, where's my treat?"

Obstacle 4: A pole weaving course (Difficulty level: 3)

How to build it: Glue five cylindrical blocks across a plywood board, standing up and staggered. For training purposes, add block walls along the sides. In fact, you can attach each course onto a separate board and later start to switch the order around for variety.

Goal: This obstacle requires your rat to weave around each pole all the way through to the end *stimulus/treat!*

1. For this one, tie a piece of string around the treat and drag it around the poles. Your rat should follow it.

2. Once your rat has gone around every single pole through to the very end, sound the stimulus and give him his reward.

3. Repeat, pulling the treat through faster, until he does it by himself.

4. If he goes around a pole the wrong (easy) way, start him on that section of the course all over again.

You may reward him for completing that one obstacle, but immediately have him run the entire course, and don't reward him until he completes it.

Obstacle 5: A seesaw (Difficulty rating: 3)

How to build it: Use carpenter's glue to attach a cylindrical wood block (fulcrum) onto a section of plywood. Next, find a rectangular block about 9" to 12" long and mark the midway point with a pencil. Use a rounded or curved file to create a semi-circular groove in the block, periodically placing it onto the fulcrum to check that it is balanced.

Goal: Teach your rat to climb up one side of the seesaw, and then down the other side. *stimulus/treat!*

1. Place a track of yogurt drops across the block. As the seesaw begins to tip from the rat's shifting weight, hold the other end of it with your hand and bring it down gently.

2. Repeat this, allowing your rat to get used to having to shift his weight.

3. When your rat gets across successfully, sound the stimulus and give him his reward.

4. Repeat several times, reducing the amount of help until your rat is finally able to walk across by himself and without following any yogurt tracks.

It may a couple weeks to master an obstacle, even longer for the more difficult ones. Learning to run an entire course may take months for your pet rats, so be patient. Once they learn the course, you may switch the order of the obstacles if you built each one on separate sections of plywood.

Finally, be sure to dip the course in a mild bleach-water solution and allow it to air-dry. Alternately, you can spray the solution on. *Dip* (don't soak) the wood, or else the glue will dissolve!

What to do if your rat escapes

It's inevitable that your rattie will slip out of his cage at some point and want to play hide and seek. Often it will come at the worst possible time! Just last week I was cleaning the cage of my two hairless beauties when one of them decided to make her great escape, running into small areas that were tough for me to get to. Unfortunately, I needed to leave for work in a half hour!

Luckily I knew exactly what to do. I'll explain.

If your rat decides to go exploring around your house, it can be tough to catch her. In fact, chasing her just makes her want to run even more, because it becomes a game! You can try all sort of tactics to coax your rat to you. (Waving a feather around so that she'll pounce on it is one idea.)

But there's an even easier way to do get her back that involves no hassle on your part. A friend of mine who's a breeder revealed the secret to me about 10 years ago.

And now I'll reveal the secret to you.

A characteristic of rats is that they have a strong nesting instinct. They know where their home is. So all you need to do is leave their cage open in their room, with the lights off. In the rest of your house, turn on all the lights.

You see, rats are nocturnal, so they'll naturally be drawn to their room. Plus, due to their nesting instincts, they'll go right back into their home. It's guaranteed. You can even put your rattie's favorite food into the cage to attract her even more.

Transporting your rat

There will be times when it will be necessary to take your rats out of your house – if you are taking a sick rat to the vet, for example. You will need to put him in a small, well-ventilated enclosure. Plastic animal carriers or even a well-ventilated cardboard box should do the trick. Don't forget to put drinking water inside, especially if the trip to the vet will be a long one.

Here are some helpful hints for making your rat's traveling experience as smooth as possible:

1. **Be forthcoming** with any hotels where you may be staying. More often than not, hotels can be very understanding, as they often host animal shows and conferences. Just be sure to adhere to their guidelines and policies.

2. **Try to be sensitive** to the fact that other people may not understand why you are traveling with a rat. Some people may be downright appalled at the idea and raise a ruckus. It's better to keep a low profile about it.

3. **If you will travel by airplane, call the airline several weeks in advance**. Their policies may range and it may take time for you to get a definite answer from their personnel. If an airline permits rat carry-ons, no doubt they will have their rules and policies. Try your best to follow them carefully.

Leaving Your Ratties Home Alone

Inevitably, there will be times when you're traveling and can't take your rats with you. As a general rule, the longest you should leave your pet rats by themselves is if you leave on an overnight trip and are back the next day.

There are many risks with leaving rats longer than that. Even if you leave a mountain of food and multiple water bottles, there's the chance that your ratties can knock over the water, go to the bathroom in their food, or even have a big feast on all that food — gorging themselves and then going diarrhea all over the cage.

Plus your rats need to have time out of their cage each day. (Remember, the minimum is 1 hour out of their cage during every 24 hour time span.) The last thing you would want would be to come home from a vacation to discover that your rats had gotten into a fight and had been bleeding. (That scenario happened to one of my friends.)

Or one of your rats could break a leg and be shivering in pain the whole time while you're gone. The bottom line is that any number of things can go wrong when you leave your ratties by themselves. And since rats can go downhill fast when they're sick or injured, it's important that someone check on them.

So if you're going to be gone for longer than 24 hours, make sure to have a friend, relative, or professional pet sitter come at least once a day to feed and play with your rats.

6. RAT HEALTH

This is perhaps the most important aspect to keeping rats. Their intelligence, attractiveness, friendliness and happiness all stem from how healthy they are.

Keeping your rats properly groomed

Most health issues can be prevented by keeping your rats clean and well groomed. While rats are very clean animals, living in a caged environment exposes them to a potentially unhealthy environment. Give your rat a bath when they become too smelly to clean themselves—for example, when they're covered in urine. (By the way, it's best to clean the cage at the same time you bathe your ratties.)

Squeeky Clean!

Usually you won't need to give your rats a traditional sort of bath, where you dunk their bodies into water. This can cause your rats a lot of stress, plus result in you getting scratched up! You see, the best cleaning solution for rats is their own tongues. (The rat's habit of self-cleaning puts even a cat to shame!) You can stimulate their own natural cleaning simply by getting them wet.

All you need to do is the following:

1. Get a shallow bowl that your rat can escape from if he needs to.
2. Fill the bowl with warm water.

3. Put some food in the water that your rat likes, but that doesn't dissolve in the water! I have the most success with grapes.

4. Let the rat dive in on his own to get the food.

If your rat doesn't dive right in, you may be using too much water. If so, just start out with a little bit of water and then gradually increase it as your rat gets used to it.

Using this warm-water-in-a-bowl method, your rat will get mostly clean just by the water rinsing him off. He'll then lick himself clean to finish the process! Make sure your rat is completely dry before putting him back into the cage.

If your rat is so dirty that he needs to be cleaned with soap, bathe him using a mild, clean-rinsing baby or pet shampoo. Dilute the shampoo with water. During the bath, you'll want to make sure not to get anything in his eyes and to get all of the shampoo off of him, since he'll groom himself afterwards.

Have a bowl full of warm water and the shampoo. Put your rat in really quick, in order to cover him with the shampoo. Then, put him into the tub to splash around. Make sure to praise your rat and give him treats in order for him to associate happy feelings with the water.

It's important that the tub be shallow enough that your rat's feet can touch the bottom. A lot of rat owners make the mistake of gripping their rat and dunking him into water against his will. This traumatizes your rat and should be avoided.

Also, remember to just bathe your rats one at a time. If you try to bathe multiple rats, you might find that you've got wet rats running around your bathroom, completely out of control!

Bathing your rats will also give you the opportunity to examine them closely. Check for any infections, injuries or tumors. Make sure their nails aren't getting too long. In the wild, their nails would normally wear down. Obviously, living in a cage all day does not allow for this, so you need to take measures to trim their nails. There's an easy way and a hard way to do this.

If you want to use clippers, do so after bath time (being super careful not to cut too close to the toe!). This will prevent accidental snags and nail injuries.

However, even if you're careful not to cut too much off, there's a chance your rat could squirm all of a sudden, causing bleeding. So, as a preventative measure, you should coat your rat's feet with an antibacterial solution and keep cotton balls or tissue nearby.

But using clippers is the hard way. Fortunately there's a much easier method. Go to the local hardware store and get a rough, flat paving stone or garden stone. Place the stone in the cage, under their water bottle. That way every time they go to get a drink of water, they scurry across the stone, which files down their nails.

Make sure to clean the stone regularly or else it will smell! Just take it out when you have your regular cage cleaning and scrub it.

Avoiding problems with your health

Before discussing rat health, it is good to become informed about the health of humans who are in the company of rats. It is common for the misinformed to believe that rats carry diseases that humans are vulnerable to. This is simply untrue, especially with domesticated rats that are kept clean.

When handling any animal (dogs and cats included!) you will want to be careful of protecting yourself from irritating germs and bacteria. Rats may, at times, bite or scratch. Allergies and rashes may develop. So, take care of scratches and rashes with antibacterial ointment. Also, a rat bite, whether deliberate or accidental, can be painful and may become infected. Don't take chances.

Good rattie health

The health risks to rats are varied. They may get into occasional scuffles, resulting in bite wounds and scratches that may be prone to infection. Their delicate tiny feet may sometimes get caught in the wires of their cage, leading to panic, struggle, and injury. If the air is too dry, they could wind up with a case of ring tail. Also, rats have been known to be prone to tumors and respiratory illnesses.

Here are the 7 magic tricks to keeping your little ones healthy:

1. Avoid dust, mites, germs and overweight issues by reviewing the "Bedding" and "Food and Water" subtopics in "Chapter 3: Getting Prepared: A Healthy Living Environment."

2. Avoid subjecting your pet rat to extremes in temperature: too hot, and they may get heatstroke; too cold, and they may get hypothermia.

3. Keep your fine furry friends away from drafts, cigarette smoke or dust.

4. After setting up their new homes, monitor them for any unforeseen health hazards or adverse reactions.

5. Keep their living areas *clean*!

6. Make sure your rats are clean. If they need a bath, bathe both of them on the same day that you clean their cage.

7. Vitamin drops can be good, but not necessary if their diet is varied and healthy. In any case, make sure your rat gets enough vitamins.

You may see some warning signs of trouble. If you notice a brownish red discharge (porphyrin, not blood) coming from their nose or eyes, it means that either their eyes and nasal passages are irritated, or they are stressed. Also, dehydration is never a good thing. Check by pulling gently on their skin and seeing if it goes back into place right away. If it doesn't, your rat is dehydrated and may need to visit the vet.

On particularly hot days, your rats may need some help staying cool. Tips to keep your rat from overheating:

1. Place ice cubes inside their water bottle.

2. Place ice cubes in a tiny bowl inside their cage. They may chew or lay on it. Discard the water soon afterwards as most likely it will be dirty.

3. Give them the option of being in a non-bedded area of their living space.

4. During play time, place a fan nearby so they can go near it (just be careful!).

Finding a veterinarian

At best, your ratties will be the lucky ones with no health issues ever; and hopefully the occasional minor sickness or injury will be treatable by you.

However, know when to say "when." If an illness becomes serious, you must be responsible enough to take your rats to the veterinarian and to spend some money on medical treatments, if needed.

In fact, you may want to search for a vet who treats rats ahead of time. That way, you will be prepared in case of an emergency.

Here is a step-by-step guide for finding the right vet for your pretty pair:

1. Find your local listings of veterinarians in the yellow pages or Internet.

2. Ask each vet if he or she will treat rats. The contact information of the ones who do will go on a short-list.

3. Go back and ask more in-depth questions:

   a. How long have you been in practice?
   b. What is your experience treating rats?
   c. How much is an office visit?
   d. Do you have a payment plan? (Most will say "no" but in the event of an emergency, what can they do if you've got a sick rat and you're strapped?)

4. You may want to eliminate the vets who have the least experience treating rats.

5. Have the cream-of-the-crop of vets send to you their brochure or web page info.

6. Keep veterinarian contact info handy at all times.

A Pet Rat First-Aid Kit

You never know when you will be faced with an emergency situation. Pet rats are just full of surprises! Don't be caught off guard. Putting a first-aid kit together ahead of time is essential for good preparedness. If you are unsure of how to use anything in your kit, consult with your vet.

The following chart has the basic medicines, tools and equipment you must have handy:

Item	Purpose	Source
Box (shoe or storage)	To store everything in	(Can be found around the house)
Critter Carrier	May double as a first-aid box	Pet store
Vet Contact info	Names and phone numbers Also include a 24-hour animal clinic	Create at home, and have it laminated at the copy store
Small face towel	To create a temporary nest	(Can be found around the house)
Hydrogen Peroxide	To clean scrapes and small wounds	Drug store
Rubbing alcohol	To sterilize skin and equipment	Drug store
Iodine	To treat wounds	Drug store
Blue Kote	To treat wounds and infections	Mail order catalog
Bag Balm	Antibiotic ointment	Pet store, Mail order catalog

Terramycin ointment	For eye irritations	Pet store, mail order catalog, vet
Ivermectin	Topical treatment for parasites	Veterinarian
Tylan Powder	Used to treat respiratory problems	Veterinarian, Mail order catalog
Cat flea powder	Add to bedding to kill parasites	Drug store, Pet store
Cat flea shampoo	A treatment for external parasites	Drug store, Pet store
Quick-stop	Stops minor bleeding	Pet store, Mail order catalog, Vet
Baking soda*	Stops minor bleeding	Drug or grocery store
Corn starch*	Stops minor bleeding	Drug store
White flour*	Stops minor bleeding	Grocery store
Q-tips	Swabbing minor wounds	Drug store
Cotton Balls	Cleaning abscesses and wounds	Drug store
Scissors	For cutting fur away from wounds	Drug store
Scalpel and sterile blades	For puncturing abscesses	Drug store, Mail order catalog
Fingernail clippers	For trimming toenails and overgrown teeth	Drug store
Eye dropper	For force-feeding, administering medicine and flushing wounds	Drug store

Syringe (without needle)	For force-feeding, administering medicine and flushing wounds	Drug store
Vick's vapo-rub	Used to mask scent when introducing unfamiliar animals to one another	Drug store
Nutrical	Nutritional supplement	Pet store, Mail order catalog
Chloroform	Use only in extreme cases when an animal must be put to sleep and no vet is available. Keep far and safely away from pets and kids.	(Illegal in some states)
Sterile gauze	For dressing drained abscesses	Drug store

*You may keep these powders handy inside of empty film canisters.

Quarantine

Most rat diseases lie dormant during an incubation period lasting 3-10 days. Although there may not be any outward signs of illness or distress, your rat may be contagious to others. Furthermore, not only does the rat carry the disease, but you, the owner, can also carry and spread the disease on your clothes.

Whenever you visit a pet store or handle unfamiliar animals, assume that they have a contagious disease. Do not handle your pets before removing your clothes and taking a very hot shower. Don't forget to wash your clothes thoroughly.

If you choose to bring a rat home from the pet store, take the following steps to quarantine him:

1. Keep your sick (or potentially sick) rat in a cage on the other side of the room, or in a separate room if possible.

2. If you come into contact with your known healthy rats, launder the clothes you were wearing and take a hot shower before handling them.

3. Keep separate from other rats for at *least* two weeks before putting them together.

Common Rat Illnesses

Mycoplasmia

This very common and incurable respiratory disease among rats may flare up throughout the rat's life. Symptoms include sneezing, wheezing and, in advanced cases, gasping for air. Sores may sometimes develop on lung tissue, making it hard for the rat to breathe. While humans are capable of catching mycoplasmia from other humans, we cannot catch it from rats, and vice versa.

There's good news though. As long as their immune system is not compromised, most rats with mycoplasmia can live long and active lives, despite the outward symptoms. The key is feeding them a vitamin-rich diet (especially vitamins A and E) and taking extra precautions to avoid exposing them to dust, smoke, drafts and bacteria.

If your rat gets "Myco flare-ups," she may need to get treated with medication such as Vibramycin, the brand name Doxycycline or the generic brand, Baytril.

These medicines will suppress symptoms and prevent the development of scarred lung tissue.

Pneumonia

The main difference between mycoplasmia and pneumonia is that the former produces symptoms of dry loud breathing that will come and go, while the latter manifests itself with a wet, congested, raspy wheeze and a runny nose. Porphyrin may be excreted from the rat's nasal passage and fluid may collect in her lungs. Babies that are infected may not show any symptoms until a few months later.

Pneumonia is highly contagious to any other rat within sneezing distance, so you should immediately quarantine the afflicted rat until you can get him to a vet.

One treatment of pneumonia involves the drugs Baytril, Doxycycline, and a machine called a nebulizer. The drugs are administered in the form of a vapor several times a day.

When and how to use cold or allergy medicine

In the event that you need to take your little one to the veterinarian to have her treated for a respiratory ailment, you may decide to administer a tiny amount of over-the-counter cold or allergy medicine.

Also, if your vet approves of the idea, you may try to treat them on your own this way over the course of several days. However, you need to be careful about doing this as you don't want to use something that may cause more harm than good. Also, if her condition should worsen, take her to a vet right away.

Here are some general guidelines:

- Use children's liquid medicines, *not* adult formulas.

- Administer the medicine as often as you would for a child; *however,* make them extremely tiny doses (0.10 cc. for an adult, and less than half that for a baby).

- Use cough decongestant or expectorant medicine, *not* suppressant.

- Avoid formulas containing alcohol.

Streptococcus Pneumonia

Strep pneumonia (*not* strep throat) is an extremely serious condition that can affect both rats and humans. Unlike other illnesses, rats can catch strep pneumonia from humans and the reverse is also true. Moreover, the disease can be fatal for rats within days of exposure. If your rat contracts strep pneumonia, it is vital that you quarantine her and seek veterinary care.

As a matter of fact, it would be wise to quarantine a pet that may have been exposed to any contagious illness or parasite. Rather than take unnecessary risks, it is better to protect your healthy household pets.

Causes of respiratory illnesses

- Bacteria from dirty cages.
- Fumes from old urine.
- Poor ventilation.
- Extreme cold.
- Drafts.

- Dust.

- Smoke.

- A combination of any of the above factors.

How to minimize respiratory illnesses and symptoms, in general:

1. Keep the air moist. Counteract the drying effect of heaters and air conditioners by adding to the room tiny water fountains, plants and even jars of water.

2. Humidifiers and vaporizers work nicely to keep the air moisture-rich; but avoid keeping them too close to your rats' cage (at *least* 4 feet away).

3. In an emergency, you can take your rat into a closed bathroom with a hot shower running. Don't take her too close to the water. Just let her breathe the steam for 5-15 minutes. It helps loosen up the mucus stuck inside their lungs.

4. Review the subtopic entitled "Bedding" in "Chapter 2: Getting Prepared: Some things to consider beforehand."

5. Sudden sneezing may be due to an allergic reaction to a change in bedding, food, soap, or to their surroundings in general.

6. A cold, tiny block of baker's chocolate has been known to ease symptoms of respiratory distress.

Abscesses and Tumors

Abscesses and tumors can be virtually indistinguishable; however, they have very different causes and consequences. Both tumors and abscesses can be life-threatening if not treated early; so if you notice a lump or abscess on your rat, you may want to play it safe and take her to the vet.

An abscess is caused by a puncture wound or irritation, such as a rat bite, that becomes increasingly infected beneath the skin. Pus collects and builds and eventually deepens and hardens.

A confident and informed pet owner can sometimes drain his pet rat's abscess at home. The pus will usually be foul-smelling. Afterwards, it is of *utmost* importance to thoroughly clean the abscessed area to prevent another one from reoccurring.

A tumor may closely resemble an abscess and similarly can gradually increase in size. As in humans, tumors can be either benign or malignant, with benign masses being the least likely to become life-threatening.

Malignant tumors, on the other hand, may develop close to vital organs and interfere with their proper functioning, resulting in death. Females get tumors, particularly mammary lumps, more often than males do.

Rats that are descended from yesterday's laboratory rats tend get lumps because their ancestors were bred for a genetic predisposition to cancer. That's one more reason to buy from a breeder! Get any tumors surgically removed as soon as possible to ensure that your pet lives a long and comfortable life.

Injuries

As babies, rats are very playful with one another. Bite wounds are not uncommon. To avoid the spread of infection, clean the wound thoroughly several times a day.

As rats age and their eyesight and agility become compromised, broken bones and sprains become common. In the case of a serious break, the vet will need to dress the wound with a bandage and administer pain killers.

It is important to keep your rats' toenails trimmed. Otherwise, they may get caught on cage wires or fabrics. To stop the bleeding, wrap the foot with a clean cloth and keep it on ice. If the bleeding doesn't stop, try to put corn-starch on it.

Tail degloving occurs when a rat's tail partially or completely breaks off. De-gloving commonly occurs if a rat is negligently pulled or picked up by the tail. To prevent this, make it a rule *never* to handle a rat by their tail. In the event that one of your rats injures her tail, you should disinfect the area well and then take her to the vet right away. A serious tail injury that goes untreated may result in a serious and possibly fatal bacterial infection.

Bumblefoot

Ulcerative Podedermatitis, more commonly known as bumblefoot, is caused by a bacterium called Staphylococcus Aureus. When rats walk over hard or wiry surfaces, they can get sores on their heels. If the sores become infected, they may develop into bumbles.

Unfortunately, bumbles are so difficult to treat. While medicine may success-fully heal the wounds, they usually will not clear up the infection itself. If your rats develop bumbles, clean their feet with a disinfecting first-aid solution sev-eral times each day.

Bumblefoot can be prevented by cleaning and disinfecting the cage and bathing your rats once every week to two weeks. Litter training also helps keep the cage less germy. Also, be sure that your rat has copious amounts of soft bedding, particularly hairless rats since their sensitive skin is particularly prone to this skin disorder.

You can help soothe the pain of bleeding bumbles by applying ice and light, steady pressure on them. Alternately, you may apply a single layer of unscented toilet paper or tissue on the bumbles.

Consult with your veterinarian for the most effective long-term treatment of bumblefoot.

Ear Infections

If you notice your rat walking around with a tilted head, it is highly likely that he has an ear infection. Other symptoms are head shaking, bad-smelling wax build up and scratching or digging at their ears. (Though digging and scratching at their ears could also indicate ear mites.) If you let these behaviors go on for too long, your rat could seriously hurt himself by puncturing his eardrum or scratching his ears to the point of infection.

To cure an ear infection, the vet will normally prescribe antibiotic drops. When administering the medicine, hold your rat's head steady for at least five minutes afterward. Otherwise, their instinct is to shake their heads and splatter the medication all over the place.

One good method of preventing ear problems is to clean your rats' ears frequently. Bath time is probably your best bet for ear-cleaning since the wax and dead skin should be softened by the bath water. However, if you do not intend on cleaning and drying your rat's ears at bath time, avoid getting their ears wet. Wet ear canals are prone to infection.

Gently wipe the outer front part of their ears using a cotton ball dipped in diluted antibacterial soap. Then, dry the ears with another cotton ball. Use a Q-tip to clean and dry the ear canals being extra careful not to push it inside too far (though rat's ear canals are usually too tiny to allow this to happen, anyway). Alternately, wet baby wipes have been known to work well.

Barbering

Barbering, power grooming or over-grooming is when your rat gnaws at her fur, creating shorn or bald patches all over her body. This behavior can suggest several mental and physical health issues, including fear, nervousness, lice, mites, fleas, or even a developing tumor.

If you notice your rat over-grooming herself, disinfect the shorn area, bathe her, and put anti-itch cream on the area. If the behavior persists, see the vet.

Symptoms of Aging

The average life expectancy for a rat is three years, with the record longest living rat reportedly dying at the ripe old age of 7, according to the Guinness Book of World Records? The oldest rat I have ever had was a male named Rodney who died at the age of 6.

This brings up the cry from rattie lovers: why must they die so soon? I've struggled with this question for almost three decades of rat ownership.

Your rat's life expectancy comes from a combination of exercise, proper nutrition, and, most of all, genetics.

The good news, however, is that there is something you can do above and beyond all of that to boost your pet rat's life expectancy, using secrets discovered very recently by medical researchers. You see, a lot of the studies aimed at boosting longevity in humans are done on rats, so it's a good idea to keep up with what is being done.

A recent huge breakthrough was the discovery that rats given a supplement called Inositol (chemical name Inositol hexaphosphate or IP6) had almost double the normal life expectancy as rats in a control group and almost never got cancer!

Inosital comes from high fiber foods such as brown rice, wheat bran and sesame seeds. The net result for your rattie is fewer cancerous tumors and a higher degree of overall health, since the study found that it aids your rattie's body in its metabolism for healthier bone marrow, liver functioning, calcium absorption, and a few other things. If you wish you can read more about this at The American Cancer Society website through this link: http://petratguide.com/acs

The best part is that you can find cheap Inositol at your local vitamin store. You see, a lot of humans believe that IP6 can help them just as it helps rats, so it's readily available.

Just dissolve one-eighth of a teaspoon per 16 ounces of water into the drinking water of your rats. Your rats will probably like the taste (my own ratties prefer it to regular water), since it tastes sweet.

Also, if the water bottle is exposed to light, cover it with aluminum foil since Inositol is sensitive to light.

Finally, if you do use Inositol with your pet rats, I recommend supplementing their diet from time to time with iron, as IP6 can slow your rattie's absorption of that mineral.

As always, be sure to double check everything with your veterinarian and check the studies I linked to for yourself, but clearly this is important news for us pet rat lovers who would do anything to boost the life expectancy of our little ratties. I've only just started my own pet rats on Inositol a couple months ago, but I'm observing initial signs of increased health that look promising

With rats, most aging symptoms are similar to those of humans. And as with people, it takes caring and patience to assist your dear rattie through her last stage of life.

The best preparation is to know what to expect. For example, old rats have the tendency to develop incontinence, urinating all over themselves. All you can really do is give them frequent baths. Otherwise, their fur will have a yellow tint and foul smell. Also, their bones and teeth can become sore; so be sure to lay down extra soft bedding and feed them soft, water-rich foods.

Putting fruits and veggies through a juicer is a great way to continue feeding them. Put the juice into their water bottle along with ice chips to keep it fresh longer. At that point, stop feeding them lab blocks.

When arranging the furniture, adapt the living environment to their abilities. Once rats get old, they are no longer able to run, climb and jump as they used to; nor are they able to recover from injuries as easily. Be sensitive to this and make their cage as safe as possible by lowering all their platforms and making their food and water available lower.

As rats age, it gets more difficult for their bodies to regulate their temperatures. That means they will be most prone to hypothermia in the winter and overheating in the summer. To keep them warm, in extremely cold weather place a heating pad or electric blanket below (not inside!) their cage. Ice cubes and a powerful fan (placed far away) can help cool an elderly rat during a heat wave.

There are other tell-tale signs of rat-aging. Once their appetites decrease, they'll lose a lot of weight. Don't be surprised if their bones begin to show. After awhile, they will become less interested in grooming themselves. As a result, their hair will be disheveled.

It is not uncommon to see a rat that is on the brink of death frantically get up and start running and hopping around in circles. On the other hand, elderly rats frequently suffer from hind leg paralysis and spend the rest of their lives falling or dragging their hind quarters around. Eventually, your rats will suddenly begin struggling to breathe, passing away within days or hours.

Dealing with the loss of your dear friend can be the most difficult part of being a pet rat owner. You gave all your love to your rat and took the best care of them that you possibly could... but your efforts were ultimately in vain. However, you did the best you could and gave your rattie the best possible life during his short time with you.

Psychologically, grief for a pet can be as overwhelming as it is for a close human relative who dies. Robin Jean Brown, author of *How to ROAR: Pet Loss Grief Recovery* has generously contributed a special mini-guide to coping with the sadness that comes from saying goodbye. You can find her guide at the end of this book.

Okay, I have a pregnant rat on my hands, now *what do I do?*

You notice your rattie's belly swelling. Even though a pet rat's belly will grow naturally after a few meals that are too big, this belly will be bigger than normal and eventually shift downward. Her nipples will probably enlarge as well.

At this point, if you've never had experience with a rat's pregnancy before, you're probably thinking, "HELP!"

First of all, take a breath. Be calm. There are a few simple rules you can follow, which will make everything go as smoothly as possible.

The normal gestation period for a rat is a short 21 to 27 days or so. In the final week before giving birth, mama will become *huge*... your friends might think she's swallowed an apple!

Shortly before giving birth, you can expect your pregnant female to make a gigantic nest out of whatever material she can get her teeth on.   Give her some napkins and paper towels she can use to make excellent bedding and nesting materials.

At the first sign of pregnancy, quarantine the mama-to-be from the other ratties. This is both for her protection and for that of the other rats – a pregnant female can become defensive and lash out at the other rats. Plus other rats can occasionally be aggressive with a pregnant female. To be on the safe side, let her have her own cage until she has given birth and the babies have been weaned.

Give her food that's packed with nutrients. There are several possibilities:

- Kitten food. Of all the commercial pet foods, kitten food is packed with the most vitamins and nutrients.
- Fresh fruits.
- Fresh veggies.
- Soy Milk.
- Baby Food.

"Aren't we cute?"

Once the babies are born, you don't need to do much other than to keep mother and children separated from your other rats. The mother takes care of everything else. Keep a vet on call, of course. After about month and a half, your little kits will be grown up enough to be able to survive without their mother's help.

Follow the rules above, and you'll almost always be fine with your rattie's pregnancy and childbirth. The most important thing is for you to not get stressed. Just about everyone who keeps at least one male and one female faces a pregnancy sooner or later.

CONCLUSION

Take care of your pet rats and, more importantly, enjoy them. They can demonstrate more love and affection in their short life spans than many humans will show you in a day. You may even find yourself wanting to get more rats!

Thank you very much for buying my guide. You will have the highest amount of happiness and a wonderful relationship with your little ratties.

Cordially,

Colin Patterson

Colin Patterson
Boston, MA
September 13, 2006

P.S. Be sure to check out rat expert Diana Davidson's free rattie secrets email newsletter. Go to http://petratguide.com/diana to find out about it and sign up.

SPECIAL BONUS CHAPTER — "WHY DID MY RAT DIE SO SOON? COPING WITH THE LOSS" By Robin Jean Brown, Author of *How to ROAR: Pet Loss Grief Recovery*

By far the toughest challenge any pet rat owner has is facing the death of their little baby. Robin Jean Brown, one of the world's foremost experts on pet loss, has contributed this chapter...

Hopefully, you read about all the precautions in Colin's guide before getting a pet rat.

According to Colin, you can maximize your rattie's life if you...

1. Buy a pair of rats from a responsible breeder.
2. Prepare a fun, clean, and loving environment for your pet rat to live in.
3. Clean and disinfect the cage or aquarium frequently.
4. Feed them healthy foods with a wide range of vegetables and fruits (including nuts and seeds).
5. Keep them away from extremely cold environments and drafts.
6. Take them out for at least a half-hour each day.
7. Care for them if they get sick, and, if necessary seek treatment from a veterinarian.

You may have followed all the proper guidelines for keeping your rat healthy and happy, but your pet rat may have died anyway. Three-year-old rats are regarded as the senior citizens of the rat world; so if the age of your rat approached the three-year mark, consider yourself blessed. If your rat was still young, it may have had a dormant genetic predisposition to an illness. It's impossible to know for sure, but this does happen every now and then.

After bonding with a furry rat friend, it can be difficult to cope with the loss. A pet rat can even be regarded as a member of your family or even a soul mate, and the end of its life can be the end of an era for the pet's owner. A lot can change for a person in the typical rat lifespan of three years, particularly when it is enriched by caring for and being loved by a pet rat.

Your friends may not understand why you feel so sad. They may even tell you horrible things like, "It was just a rat. Get over it." The fact is, you can't just "get over it." Your rattie was not "just a rat." And it's totally normal for you to go through a long period of mourning and grieving.

In fact, according to veterinarian Dr. Marc Rosenberg, grief over the loss of a pet can strongly resemble the grief that one feels over the loss of a close human friend or family member.

Understand that your friends may not truly understand what you're going through. We live in a society that can be insensitive, as it does not typically support people in their grieving process over their pets. A pet owner may feel embarrassment or even frustration at having to hear insensitive remarks such as "Come on, it was *only* a rat!" and "You can always go buy another one." Please remember that people tell you such things in a misguided attempt to help you, not because they're being intentionally cruel.

So make no mistake... grief over the loss of a pet can be very real. One effective way of coping is to simply be familiar with the various stages of grief. It also helps to know that all the feelings are healthy and, in time, they will ease. Finally, whenever you feel ready, you can decide to make a donation to a humane organization or scholarship fund in your pet rat's memory.

The Mourning Process

Here are the main stages of the grieving process first identified in a book called *On Death and Dying* by Dr. Kubler-Ross:

DENIAL

On a subconscious level, denial is a mechanism that helps a person to prepare for the trauma of learning about a pet's illness or sudden death. It takes time to allow the truth to "sink in." At this time, it is helpful to read literature on the nature of the animal's disease.

BARGAINING

Whether subconsciously or not a person can often go through a phase when he is "willing to do anything" to make his pet well or bring him back. Sometimes, this phase is skipped altogether. Taken to extremes this stage is illogical but is, nonetheless, a normal part of grief.

ANGER

Next, there is a point in which the pet owner wants to find someone to blame for the loss. This can manifest itself as hostility expressed toward the veterinarian or family member. Alternately or simultaneously, the pet owner can feel guilt, a harmful, inwardly-directed form of anger.

Outward forms of hostility require compassion and understanding from others. Feelings of guilt will require the grieving individual to try to recall all the positive actions that were taken to care for the pet.

GRIEF

Once denial has given way to acceptance and once the anger and guilt have subsided, the feeling that remains is pure grief. In this stage, the pet owner deals with the sadness and the void left behind by the loss. It is at this stage that the pet owner needs the most support. Otherwise, this period may be prolonged for several years. At this phase of grief, buying or adopting a new pet can be a way to ease the pain or fill the void.

The following is normal for a person who is experiencing grief:

- Disturbed sleep patterns
- Decreased work efficiency
- Affected appetite

At times when it may be particularly difficult, a pet owner may require professional assistance in expressing his emotions. Searching for a pet-loss support group may help. A local Veterinary school or centers may provide just the kind of support needed.

RESOLUTION

This final stage of the grieving process occurs when strong emotions subside. The pet owner is finally able to look at pictures and recall the past without pain. If a new pet is acquired, it is to add a new member to the household, not to fill an emptiness left by the previous pet's absence.

It is not uncommon for the pet owner to experience a relapse further into the resolution process; however, this usually lasts for a brief time after which the griever returns to the resolution phase, stronger than before.

Euthanasia

In the case of having to euthanize your dear pet rat, strong feelings of grief can come particularly early. How you deal with the entire process depends on a variety of factors including: the degree of your attachment to him, your grief responses to previous deaths, and how much has been processed at the actual moment of putting your pet to sleep.

To a degree, putting animals to sleep is difficult for the veterinarian as well, particularly if there was a tremendous life-saving effort involved. Therefore, keeping the lines of communication open is the key to handling the ordeal in as positive and a manner as possible.

The two main issues addressed in euthanizing a pet is how humane the procedure is for the animal and how comfortable it is for you, the pet owner. This may require some flexibility on the part of the veterinarian and a great deal of support for you by the way of information regarding your choices.

Keeping your rat company while he is being put to sleep can be a difficult choice to make. However, knowing that you were there to comfort your little guy during his last moments can help you process your grief. Here is an overview of both possibilities:

Accompanying your pet rat as he is being put to sleep

Owners who choose not to be with their pets can often feel pangs of guilt, afterward, to imagine that their little friend may have felt abandoned and frightened.

On the other hand, an extreme emotional response on your part such as crying loudly, or even fainting, can place a burden on both your pet and the clinician.

A nervous rat on the euthanizing table can end up interfering with the procedure. A struggle may ensue, making the experience even more traumatic than deemed necessary.

Usually, veterinarians have guidelines for involving pet owners as their pets are being "put down." For the reasons that were previously discussed, veterinarians often prefer to be alone with your pet while the catheter is being inserted into the rat's vein.

Once the administering of the drug is about to begin, the vet may invite you into the room to comfort and keep your rat company. You may speak softly to him and stroke his head as he gently drifts off. To reduce the amount of trauma, you may wish to cover your deceased rat with a blanket or towel once he is pronounced dead.

You may choose to spend a few moments with your rat's body, but try to be mindful that your vet and the animal clinic have other pets and owners to attend to.

Staying outside of the room as your pet rat is being put to sleep

Most of the time, being with a pet as he is being put to sleep can be too traumatic for a pet owner. If you feel this way, you may wish to sit in the waiting room during the actual euthanization. Your vet will likely allow you to see your little guy one last time after the procedure has ended. Doing this can help you have closure.

What to do with your pet's body?

Your pet's veterinarian is the best source of information for disposal options. Deciding the right method for you can help with the grieving process. Here are a few options with a brief overview on each:

Burial in a cemetery

The concept of the ritual burial of pets dates back to Egyptian times. Furthermore, pet cemeteries can be found throughout the US and Europe.

If your pet felt like "part of the family" and "almost human," then burial in a pet cemetery can be most appropriate. Here are a few benefits to this choice:

- The physical ritual of burial can help to bring closure
- It may be comforting to know the location of your pet's final resting place
- It provides a place where you can visit your departed friend.

A possible drawback of pet burial is the cost. The minimum cost to bury a pet is $200 for a simple burial; the cost of a more elaborate funeral can go up into the thousands of dollars. You can either make the funeral arrangements through your veterinarian or directly with the pet cemetery.

Pet cemeteries will usually offer the option of having a communal burial; this can be the most inexpensive and simplest option. If you are considering this option, ask questions and even personally investigate the practices of several cemeteries and burial services. This way, you can be reassured that your departed little rattie will be in good hands.

Cremation

Individual cremation is becoming more popular, ending in a private ash-scattering ritual at the pet owner's home. The cost can be higher than communal burial, yet more affordable than an individual pet burial.

The most economical choice for pet disposal is communal cremation. Just be sure that you understand that your furry friend's body will be burned with several other animals. The cost is usually less than $100. Ask questions regarding what is important to you so that you may ensure that you are comfortable with this option.

Home Burial

Burying your dear rattie somewhere on your own property can be a perfectly acceptable option if you have the land on which to do this. The drawback is that if you move, you would have to leave the grave behind. If you choose the route of home burial, place your rat's remains in a thick bag encased by a snug-fitting coffin or container. In this way, you will reduce the likelihood of animals following the scent of your dead rat, and digging up his remains.

Necropsy

In many cases, the vet can arrange for to determine your rat's cause of death. However, keep in mind that this test can be expensive and oftentimes the laboratory will not return your rat's body to you.

You can find out about Robin Jean Brown's guide to coping with the pet loss mourning at <u>PetLossGuide.com</u>.

© 2006 John Alexander Enterprises, Inc. Unauthorized duplication, copying, or transmission is prohibited.

Last But Definitely Not Least...

If you're ready to continue your education about pet rats, there is a free e-course and email newsletter by a young author named Diana Davidson, who has become one of the world's foremost experts on rats.

Go sign up for her free course by going to:

http://petratguide.com/diana

Register right now and you'll get private access to Diana's valuable email course, which will help you take the secrets and insights you've learned already to the next level.

However, I've heard that Diana may be closing the program soon (since there are only a limited number of slots she's going to give away at no cost), so hurry up and sign up:

http://petratguide.com/diana

About the Author

Born and raised in New England, Colin Patterson has been involved with rat and small animal rescue and has been a rat and small animal trainer, breeder and consultant for almost three decades.

He and his wife split time between Boston, Massachusetts and Athens, GA and are owned by 17 pet rats, 5 ferrets, 5 gerbils, 2 rabbits, 12 guinea pigs, 2 hamsters, 1 chinchilla and 4 pet mice.

Colin has also written a book called Find Out About Ferrets: The Complete Guide to Turning Your Ferret Into the Happiest, Best-Trained and Healthiest Pet in the World! which you can find at http://findoutaboutferrets.com

Printed in Great Britain
by Amazon.co.uk, Ltd.,
Marston Gate.